United Arab Emirates

Cavendish
Square
New York

Published in 2022 by Cavendish Square Publishing, LLC
243 5th Avenue, Suite 136, New York, NY 10016
Copyright © 2022 by Cavendish Square Publishing, LLC

Third Edition

Website: cavendishsq.com

This publication represents the opinions and views of the author based on his or her personal experience, knowledge, and research. The information in this book serves as a general guide only. The author and publisher have used their best efforts in preparing this book and disclaim liability rising directly or indirectly from the use and application of this book.

All websites were available and accurate when this book was sent to press.

Library of Congress Cataloging-in-Publication Data

Names: King, David C., author. | Mikoley, Kate, author.
Title: United Arab Emirates / David C. King and Kate Mikoley.
Other titles: Cultures of the world (third edition)
Description: Third edition. | New York : Cavendish Square Publishing, 2022.
 | Series: Cultures of the world | Includes bibliographical references
 and index.
Identifiers: LCCN 2021012392 | ISBN 9781502662675 (library binding) | ISBN
 9781502662682 (ebook)
Subjects: LCSH: United Arab Emirates--Juvenile literature.
Classification: LCC DS247.T8 K55 2022 | DDC 953.57--dc23
LC record available at https://lccn.loc.gov/2021012392

Writers: David C. King; Kate Mikoley, third edition
Editor, third edition: Kate Mikoley
Designer, third edition: Jessica Nevins

PICTURE CREDITS

Some of the images in this book illustrate individuals who are models. The depictions do not imply actual situations or events.

CPSIA compliance information: Batch #CS22CSQ: For further information contact Cavendish Square Publishing LLC, New York, New York, at 1-877-980-4450.

Printed in the United States of America

Find us on

CONTENTS

UNITED ARAB EMIRATES TODAY

N **ESTLED BETWEEN THE PERSIAN GULF, THE GULF OF OMAN, OMAN,** and Saudi Arabia lies one of the wealthiest countries in the world. It is a union of seven small emirates, or kingdoms. Together, these kingdoms make up the United Arab Emirates (UAE).

The part of the world now known as the UAE has a long and rich history, but before the 1950s, the small country was largely unknown to many people around the world. Once oil was found in the region, that all changed. With the discovery of oil, one of the world's most valuable commodities, the economy of the UAE boomed. Today, it is among the most important economic centers in the world.

The country is dry and hot, and most of the land is desert. However, with more than 800 miles (1,300 kilometers) of coastline, much of the country is also made up of beautiful beaches. With high temperatures all year long and very little rain, the UAE has become a top tourist destination for those looking for a relaxing beach vacation. The nation's thriving cities are home to some of the world's tallest buildings, fanciest hotels, and most fascinating people.

THE EMIRATES

The largest of the country's emirates is Abu Dhabi, also the capital of the UAE. In fact, Abu Dhabi is so large, it takes up about three-fourths of the country's, or federation's, total land. The next largest emirate is Dubai, also sometimes spelled Dubayy. The capital city of the emirate of Dubai is the city of Dubai. This important port city is home to hundreds of global corporations, many impressive skyscrapers, and the majority of the emirate's population. In fact, more than nine-tenths of the people living in the emirate of Dubai live in or directly around the city of Dubai.

The federation's five smallest emirates are Sharjah (also spelled Al-Shāriqah), ʻAjmān, Umm al-Qaywayn, Ra's al-Khaymah, and al-Fujayrah. Al-Fujayrah is the only of the country's seven emirates to have no land along the Persian Gulf. Instead, the emirate faces the Gulf of Oman.

This photo shows the skyline of the capital city of the emirate of Sharjah. The city is also called Sharjah.

GOVERNMENT

An emir is what a ruler, commander, or chief is called in an Islamic country. An emirate is the land over which an emir rules or commands. Each of the UAE's emirates has its own ruler, government, courts, and police force. The Federal Supreme Council, the highest government authority in the UAE, is made up of each of the seven emirate's rulers. The Supreme Council elects one member to be president and one member to be vice president of the federation, each for a term of five years. It is the president's job to appoint a prime minister and a cabinet.

The country's unicameral legislature is called the Federal National Council. This council is made up of 40 advisory members, each appointed by an emirate for a two-year term. Similar to the United States, the UAE has laws set forth by a constitution. Also like the United States, any powers not given to the federal government in the constitution are powers of the individual emirates.

ECONOMY AND TOURISM

The economy in the United Arab Emirates depends heavily on oil and natural gas sales. However, tourism is also now a big part of the country's economy. In fact, the tourism and oil industries go hand in hand for the UAE. Oil, first discovered in the area in 1958, changed everything for the region we now know as the United Arab Emirates. Money made from the sales of the oil helped to improve the land, making it more hospitable to citizens and visitors alike. Such improvements have helped the country become a top vacation destination, with tourists from all over the world traveling to see the country's impressive beaches, cities, and cultural destinations. Money made from the sale of oil and gas has also improved other areas of the economy. As improvements were made to the land and cities were built up, more multinational corporations chose to make the United Arab Emirates an important home base. Thus, parts of the country have become key business and financial centers.

The United Arab Emirates has some of the most unique infrastructure and architecture in the world today.

THE PEOPLE

Perhaps one of the most surprising facts about the United Arab Emirates is that most of the people living there are not citizens of the country. Most are actually people from other countries who are in the United Arab Emirates to work. Only about 12 percent of the country's people are citizens of the United Arab Emirates. Those who are native to or citizens of the UAE are commonly known as Emiratis.

Most people living in the UAE live in cities along the coast. The largest group of people living in the UAE are those from South Asia. The next largest population group is made up of people from Arab countries outside of the United Arab Emirates. Arabic is the official language of the United Arab Emirates, although several other languages, including English, are also widely spoken here.

About three-fifths of the people in the UAE are Muslim. The majority of the country's Muslim population belongs to the Sunni branch of Islam, although there are also members of the Shia branch, mainly living in Dubai and Sharjah. In recent years, Christian and Hindu communities have also begun to grow in the country. With people from many different parts of the world now calling it home, the United Arab Emirates is a country brimming with cultural diversity.

GEOGRAPHY

Some of the world's largest sand dunes are located in the deserts of the UAE.

1

OIL HAS PLAYED A LARGE ROLE IN just about every area of the United Arab Emirates' development—and that includes the country's geography. Harsh desert environments, such as the one that makes up most of the UAE, can be hard to survive in and are certainly difficult for many people to thrive in. However, the discovery of oil and the subsequent increase in the country's wealth have changed the people's relationship with the land. What once was a long journey through hot, sandy desert land can now be a quick trip down a highway divided by lush, hydrated greenery. A line of trees helps keep back what once would have made the journey unbearable—strong, hot gusts of sand.

The country's seven small emirates lie in the southeastern corner of the Arabian Peninsula. To the west and south, the nation is bordered by Saudi Arabia. To the east and northeast is the country of Oman. To the

The UAE is located on the Arabian Peninsula, which also includes Saudi Arabia, Yemen, Oman, Kuwait, Qatar, and Bahrain.

north, the country's coastline touches the Persian Gulf, while a small section of the northeast part of the country borders the Gulf of Oman.

Together, all of the emirates in the UAE take up only slightly more than 32,000 square miles (82,880 sq km). To put that into perspective, that's slightly smaller than the size of Maine in the United States. The state of Florida is more than twice the size of the UAE. Though mainly made up of sandy desert, there are also mountains, wetlands, and coastal plains.

COASTAL LIVING

With most people living along the waters and ports, which are key locations for the country's oil trade, the coast is an important feature of the United Arab Emirates. Though most of the federation is desert, a narrow coastal strip is semifertile, especially when properly irrigated. Additionally, large portions of the coast are made up of salt flats, called *sabkhah*, which formed over thousands of years as wind eroded and shifted the sand dunes. The salt flats form a belt 200 miles (320 km) long along the coast.

The coast itself is a mixture of reefs, shoals, lagoons, and low-lying islands. There are more than 200 islands off the coast. Some are privately owned by the ruling sheikhs. There are no natural, deepwater harbors on the Persian Gulf coast of the UAE, but the country has worked around this by constructing artificial harbors. In addition, there are three good, natural harbors on the Gulf of Oman.

In the south, the emirate of Abu Dhabi lies on the edge of the notorious Rub' al-Khali, also known as the Empty Quarter—the largest area of continuous sand in the world. Covering an area of 250,000 square miles (650,000 sq km), the Empty Quarter is nearly as large as the U.S. state of Texas. To the north, however, Abu Dhabi meets the Persian Gulf for about 280 miles (450 km) of coastline.

INTO THE OASES AND WADIS

Oases are often perceived as backyard-sized islands of green in an ocean of sand. However, oases actually vary greatly in size, and some are surprisingly large. The oasis of al-Buraymi, for example, includes Al-'Ayn, a city of 200,000 people.

These oases have been vital to desert survival for centuries, especially in the past, when a camel caravan might have spent two weeks crossing a stretch of desert. In addition to al-Buraymi, UAE's oases include Liwa, a fertile crescent of more than 50 separate oases. In the past 30 years, water from desalination plants and more modern irrigation systems have helped to maintain the lush greenery.

Riverbeds, called wadis in mountain regions, have also been important farming regions for many centuries. The country's upland wadis support such crops as wheat, sorghum, and alfalfa, plus a variety of fruits, including mangoes, bananas, limes, and grapes. The UAE is one of the world's leading producers of dates, and date palms thrive in wadis and around oases.

THE COUNTRY'S SEVEN EMIRATES

Since formally coming together as one nation in 1971, the UAE has displayed a remarkable degree of unity. At the same time, however, each emirate retains its own unique identity. They also differ greatly in size, population, and geographical features.

Abu Dhabi is by far the largest of the emirates, covering around 28,000 square miles (73,000 sq km), which is more than 80 percent of the total land area of the federation. The UAE's capital city, also named Abu Dhabi, is situated on an island connected to the mainland by a causeway. Much of the emirate's land is desert, but Abu Dhabi includes the major oasis areas of Al-'Ayn, Liwa, and al-Buraymi, on the border with Oman.

Abu Dhabi is also the center of the country's oil industry, holding more than 95 percent of the UAE's proven oil reserves and 92 percent of its gas reserves. This, along with the city of Abu Dhabi being the country's capital, has made it the dominant emirate, both politically and economically.

Wadis are often home to groups of trees, including date palms and other fruit trees.

MIGHTY MOUNTAINS

You might not think of a small, mostly desert country on the coast as having many mountains, but the UAE does. While the al-Hajar Mountains are mainly in Oman, they also reach into the eastern part of the UAE. They act as a divide between the coast and the desert. The city of Dubai is not far from the base of these mountains. The peaks average about 4,000 feet (1,200 meters) in elevation, but the highest ones within the UAE reach as high as 6,500 feet (2,000 m). Even higher peaks exist in the chain outside of the UAE. What little rain falls here drains from these mountains into the wadis nearby. Archaeologists have found evidence that these mountain regions were once important centers of civilization, with remains from such towns dating back thousands of years.

Dubai, the second largest emirate, is significantly smaller than Abu Dhabi, covering about 1,500 square miles (3,900 sq km). The emirate's capital city, also called Dubai, is the largest city within the UAE. As a port city, Dubai is a hub for business, but it is also a popular tourist destination. While Abu Dhabi dominates politically and in terms of oil wealth, the emirate of Dubai has considerable oil revenue of its own and has been the commercial hub of the country for many years. It is often regarded as the most modern and freewheeling of all the emirates.

Sharjah is the third largest emirate at about 1,000 square miles (2,600 sq km). While it is often overshadowed by Abu Dhabi and Dubai, things have started to change in more recent years. The ruling family has used the shared oil wealth and its own small quantity of light-grade oil to modernize the city of Sharjah and to establish modern roads, schools, and health-care facilities. In spite of its 21st-century look, Sharjah also shows remnants of its long history in the form of ancient forts and watchtowers, including a waterfront lined with dhows, the traditional boats used for fishing, pearl diving, and trade.

Together, the three small emirates of 'Ajmān, Umm al-Qaywayn, and Ra's al-Khaymah cover about as much area as Sharjah. 'Ajmān, the smallest emirate, covers only about 100 square miles (260 sq km). It is located between the

Persian Gulf and Sharjah. Many pearl divers once sailed from its port, but today the port contains a long wharf used to repair boats that supply the UAE's oil fields. The fertile soil in the mountains of 'Ajmān also makes it a producer of vegetables and citrus fruits.

Umm al-Qaywayan, with an area of 300 square miles (780 sq km), is the second smallest emirate in size. It is also the least populous, with an estimated population of less than 50,000 people. During the heat of the day, the streets of its main town are practically deserted. The offshore island of al-Siniyyah is a wildlife sanctuary with large populations of nesting herons, as well as cormorants, turtles, and sea snakes, while the sea cows called dugongs swim in the shallow waters. Archaeological excavations show that people have fished and hunted there for more than 5,000 years.

Ra's al-Khaymah, which covers an area of 660 square miles (1,700 sq km), is the most fertile of the emirates, with groves of date palms as well as grazing areas for sheep and cattle. It also has varied marine life.

Finally al-Fujayrah, the most remote of the emirates, is the only one with no land on the Persian Gulf. Instead, it faces the Gulf of Oman. At 500 square miles (1,300 sq km), it is located to the east of Dubai. Although it is one of the poorer of the emirates, al-Fujayrah has some excellent agricultural land and has become important for raising poultry and dairy cattle.

A HOT CLIMATE

The climate of the UAE is, for the most part, hot and humid along the coast and still hotter, but dry, inland. The average January temperature is around 65 degrees Fahrenheit (18 degrees Celsius). By July, the average temperature is close to 95ºF (35ºC). However, temperatures can reach as high as 115ºF (46ºC) on the coast and 120ºF (49ºC) inland. In midwinter and early summer, winds known as the *shamal* blow from the north and northwest carrying unwelcomed sand and dust. Rainfall rarely measures more than 3 to 4 inches (75 to 100 millimeters) in a year. Not surprisingly, streets and wharfs are quite empty in the early afternoon, at least in summer, and construction workers do much of their work in the early mornings and evenings. To make scorching

hot cities more comfortable, there has been extensive planting of trees and grass, as well as creation of numerous parks and fountains. Widespread air-conditioning also makes the cities much more comfortable.

PLANTS THAT THRIVE

Despite the hot and dry weather, the country's plant and animal life is surprisingly varied, and the government's efforts to draw tourists make use of this variety. The deserts are home to several endangered species, and efforts have been made to protect and expand these populations. In terms of plants, many hardy varieties of tropical and subtropical trees and other flora have been added alongside indigenous species.

While the desert of the UAE is a harsh place where most plants struggle to survive, many grasses, bushes, and other low-growing plants thrive there. Such plants include the desert squash, desert hyacinth, firebush, and Sodom's apple. Coastal areas and oases have a variety of plants and grasses as well.

Trees are particularly important to the UAE and the people who live there. In fact, the UAE has been celebrating Tree Week in mid-April every year since 1981. Among the trees commonly found in parks and urban greenbelts is the Gulmohar, often called the *fleur de paradis*, a native plant from Madagascar, enjoyed for its orange and red blossoms. The portia tree, also called the umbrella tree, is also common. The tree has small yellow flowers and small apple-like fruit, which are used to produce yellow dyes. The wood and bark are used to make a red dye.

Other trees with practical uses include the frywood, whose bark is used in the manufacture of medicines. This tree has papery, yellow pods that noisily

Dates are an important food and income source for the people of the UAE.

clack together. The margosa, also called the neem tree, produces hundreds of tiny yellow flowers. The blossoms, along with the leaves, roots, and bark, are also used in the production of medicines.

Perhaps the most important tree in the UAE is the date palm. These trees are native to the region. The fruits they produce, which range in color from pale yellow to deep red, hang in large clusters, often 3 feet (0.9 m) in length. The trees thrive in oases, where the water table is close to the surface. Ancient irrigation channels, called *falaj*, carry water from underground springs to date palm groves.

For centuries, the date palm was vital to desert survival. The fruit it produced was a staple of the Emirati diet, and its trunk and leaves were used to make a variety of household items and small boats. Date palm leaves were also used to make *barasti* houses, which were common before concrete was available. A barasti house had a wooden frame and supports with walls, room dividers, and a roof made of palm leaves. The leaves were also used to make a four-sided wind tower at the top of the house, which directed cooling breezes into the rooms below. While household items, boats, and houses are now often made from other materials, the date palm remains important to the culture of the UAE.

Today it is estimated that there are more than 40 million date palms in the UAE. Due to the abundance of dates, many people in the UAE eat them daily. Special guests and visitors are often treated to the best dates available. Date farming is also incredibly important to the UAE economy, and many people make their livelihoods working on date farms. The country is among the top exporters of dates in the world. In 2018, the Sixth International Date Palm Conference was held in Abu Dhabi. Date palm experts from around the world gathered to share ideas and discuss the state of date palm farming and cultivation.

ANIMAL LIFE

Each small region of the UAE has its own unique animal life, including birds, reptiles, and a number of rare species of larger animals. One of the many surprises of this fascinating desert country is that it is a conducive place

AN ISLAND SANCTUARY

In the early 1970s, the founder of the UAE, Sheikh Zāyid ibn Sulṭān Al Nahyān, visited an abandoned island about 150 miles (241 km) southwest of Abu Dhabi. At the time, the island was rocky and had no trees or fresh water. After seeing it for himself, Sheikh Zāyid decided the island should be turned into a nature preserve. Today, the island, called Sir Bani Yas, is home to thousands of animals and millions of trees. Many of the animals on the island are endangered or were once close to extinction. The island has helped preserve these species, and breeding programs have even helped the growth of some populations, such as those of the Arabian oryx and the Arabian gazelle. Sir Bani Yas, today part of the emirate of Abu Dhabi, is also a popular tourist attraction, home to a resort that offers safari adventures for guests.

Visitors take photos of wildlife as they drive to the safari park on Sir Bani Yas.

for bird-watching, an activity that many people participate in. The country's determined effort to increase parkland and green space has led to a steady increase in birdlife. An additional factor is that the UAE is situated on one of the planet's main migration routes. Up to 300 species stop over there on their way to or from Europe, Africa, and Asia.

In addition, several areas in the UAE have organizations called Natural History Groups, which engage in spotting and recording information about birds. The groups are especially active in autumn and spring—the best seasons for bird sightings. Bird-watchers have spotted hundreds of species nesting, migrating, or wintering. Safa Park, a few miles outside the city of Dubai, has proven to be an excellent site for the hobbyists. Of the 230 species recorded there, some are common, such as the robin and thrush, but there are also gray shrikes, European bee-eaters, and many warblers, including the great reed warbler. Dubai Creek and the shallow lake attract pintail ducks and many waders. Beach areas and the islands draw even more varieties, including plovers, herons, flamingos, terns, and egrets.

Several animal species that were once desert dwellers are now found primarily in reserves such as Sir Bani Yas. These include the Gordon's wildcat and the striped hyena. A few species, such as the red fox and Blanford's fox, manage to survive even in extreme conditions. In addition, there are several insectivores—mammals that feed on insects. These include the shrew

The desert hedgehog can be found in many parts of the Arabian Peninsula. This one is in Sharjah.

and several kinds of hedgehogs. In addition, the UAE deserts are also host to several bat species, in particular the Egyptian fruit bat.

Not surprisingly, the desert environment is a comfortable habitat for many species of reptiles. More than 50 varieties have been recorded in the UAE, including many kinds of lizards, which are more common than snakes. Snake species include the desert boa, the sand snake, the Arabian rear-fang, and the sand viper, which buries itself in sand up to its eyes and nostrils.

LIFE IN THE WATER

People living on the coasts have relied on fishing for centuries for food and jobs. The Persian Gulf is home to schools of mackerel, grouper, tuna, and others, as well as sharks and occasionally whales. Additionally, dhow excursions that take visitors on dolphin watches are a popular tourist activity.

Abu Dhabi has the second largest population of dugongs in the world, after Australia. A dugong is a type of sea cow related to the manatee. It is estimated that about 7,300 of them live in the Persian Gulf, and about 3,000 live in the waters of Abu Dhabi.

There are also a number of coral reefs off the coast of the UAE. The colorful tropical fish living among the coral have made scuba diving a favorite activity for locals and tourists alike. Not all coral reefs are completely natural, however. Over the years, climate change and development have caused damage to sea life all over the world, including near the UAE. In 2020, divers were working off the east coast of the UAE to help change that. To do this, the divers cut off pieces of coral reef and replanted it in other parts of the water. The idea is that this helps more coral grow, restoring the reefs and creating a rich habitat for marine life. However, this can't happen overnight. Over a year's time, the divers planted about 9,000 corals, covering an area of about 6,458 square feet (600 sq m). Their goal is to plant 1.5 million corals over an area of more than 3 million square feet (300,000 sq m) over a period of five years. Even so, it could take up to 15 years for meaningful amounts of coral to be growing naturally in the area.

LAND OF GROWTH

Despite being a relatively small country in size, the United Arab Emirates is home to a diverse array of plant and animal life. The country has also implemented initiatives to help make the harsh desert area that makes up most of the land more hospitable to these plants and animals—as well as the people who call the United Arab Emirates home. Within the past few decades, the country known for its hot and dry climate has seen great growth in plant and animal life thanks to efforts to help preserve and protect important species, as well as growth in tourism thanks, in part, to the country's stunning geographical features.

INTERNET LINKS

www.nationalgeographic.com/travel/article/sir-bani-yas-united-arab-emirates
This article has photos and information about the island of Sir Bani Yas.

www.thoughtco.com/geography-of-united-arab-emirates-1435701
This page has an array of facts about the United Arab Emirates, including about its geography and climate.

www.worldatlas.com/maps/united-arab-emirates
View several maps of the United Arab Emirates and learn more about the country's geography on this website.

HISTORY

DUBAI MUSEUM

The Dubai Museum, located inside the Al Fahidi Fort, showcases much about the history of life in Dubai.

2

T HE HISTORY OF THE PART OF THE world we now know as the United Arab Emirates dates back thousands of years, but everything changed with the discovery of oil in the 20th century. In fact, some would say in order to best understand the nation's past, it should actually be split up into two separate histories: before oil discovery and after oil discovery. The earlier history looks quite different from the nation we know as the UAE today. However, the early history sets the stage for the story of growth that is the nation's recent history. To many observers, it appears that no nation in the world has changed as greatly or quickly as the UAE has since oil was discovered there.

"He who does not know his past cannot make the best of his present and future, for it is from the past that we learn."
—Sheikh Zāyid ibn Sulṭān Al Nahyān, founder and first president of the UAE

EARLY HUMAN HISTORY

Evidence shows that human groups have inhabited the area that is now known as the UAE for more than 7,000 years. Archaeological findings

indicate that Stone Age people living there used simple tools for farming, growing crops of wheat, barley, and palm dates from 3000 BCE. They also raised cattle, sheep, and goats. There is also evidence that by 2500 BCE, camels were likely domesticated and were probably used in establishing inland settlements at wadis and oases. In addition, trade items such as pottery and copper were being shipped to the early civilizations of Mesopotamia. In other words, a well-developed maritime trade was already an important part of the regional economy as early as 2000 BCE.

After 300 BCE, in the centuries following the death of Alexander the Great, what is now the UAE was part of a trade network linking the Mediterranean world, including ancient Greece and Rome, with the cultures of the Indian Ocean and Africa. At the same time, camel caravans, bearing goods such as frankincense, made their way north through western Arabia, while the coastal communities continued to rely on maritime trade. The people of the region used dhows of all sizes to export such goods as pearls, wood, and limestone marble.

MORE PEOPLE ARRIVE

Sometime after 200 BCE, tribes of Arab peoples began moving into the region that is now known as the UAE. Some settled in coastal areas, while others sought the fertile inland wadis and oases. Initially, the Arab tribes fought with other groups living there, who were likely of Persian descent. Gradually, over several centuries, the two groups merged, with the original settlers being absorbed into the Arab tribal structure.

The new religion of Islam swept through the region in the years after 630 CE. The religion's founder was the Arab Prophet Muhammad. God's (Allah's) words, as revealed to Muhammad, are contained in the Quran (or Koran), the holy book of Islam. In Islam, Allah is the one and only god. The spread of the religion began during Muhammad's lifetime, and its expansion accelerated after his death in 632 CE. Over the next three centuries, the religion spread across North Africa and Asia, reaching into India and the islands of the western Pacific. Today, Islam is the majority religion in the countries around the Persian Gulf.

SHEIKHS AND SHEIKHDOMS

Over the centuries, various Arab tribes and their sheikhs, or leaders, came to rule in specific areas. By the 1700s, for example, one tribe, the Bani Yas, controlled the town of Abu Dhabi and the oases of Al-'Ayn and Liwa. People were loyal to their tribe and its sheikh, rather than to a place or a country. These loyalties remain strong today. An early ruling family of the Bani Yas, the Al Nahyān family, continues to head the government of Abu Dhabi. As of 2021, the leader of Abu Dhabi and the president of the UAE is Sheikh Khalīfah ibn Zāyid Al Nahyān, the oldest son of the country's founder and former leader, Sheikh Zāyid ibn Sulṭān Al Nahyān.

Similarly, the emirate of Dubai was established under another branch of the Bani Yas. Dubai, which had existed as a town before 1580, was built along the banks of its creek, which offered one of the best anchorages for ships in the region. Ships from Persia, Pakistan, India, and other countries used its wharfs; many crew members from these ships remained in Dubai and quickly assimilated into the increasingly multicultural coastal society.

The northern emirates were dominated by the Qawasim clan, part of the powerful Huwalah tribe. The Qawasim became a sea power in the 1700s, and their growing strength was a threat to Great Britain, which resulted in clashes with the powerful British fleet. Another large and powerful tribal group, the Sharqiyyin, was spread across what is now al-Fujayrah. The followers of the sheikh eked out a living by fishing, cultivating date palms, and sea trading.

A CENTER FOR TRADE

Trade between the Mediterranean world and Asia, including China, India, and the Spice Islands, developed during the eras of the Greek and Roman empires. Coastal villages on the Persian Gulf became midway stops in this

The pearl diving industry was important to the Persian Gulf sheikhdoms for more than 2,000 years, reaching its peak in the early 1900s, when more than 400 pearling dhows were based at Abu Dhabi, about one-third of the emirate's total fleet. Around 22,000 men were involved in the industry, a great percentage of the population at that time.

Diving for pearls was a grueling and dangerous job. The men were at sea for up to four months, during the hottest months of the year. They dove on empty stomachs to avoid cramps, and they faced the constant danger of attacks by jellyfish, sharks, and sea snakes. The work was sometimes very profitable, and this attracted men who had few other opportunities for work.

The pearling industry was mostly destroyed in the 1930s, when the Japanese learned the secret of cultivating cultured pearls. The economic chaos caused by the Great Depression in the 1930s added an extra blow.

This Pearl Monument in Sharjah pays tribute to the pearling industry in the United Arab Emirates.

long-distance exchange, and by the eighth century CE, Arab dhows and seamen were becoming key players in the global game of trade.

Being a maritime trader was hard and dangerous. The men spent months at sea, crammed onto open ships that were little more than floating cargo bins, with the crew living as best they could on top of the cargo. The Italian explorer Marco Polo was shocked to find that the planks of the dhows were not nailed together, but instead were stitched with twine made of coconut fiber. The construction, he wrote, "makes it a risky undertaking to sail in these ships. And you can take my word that many of them sink because the Indian Ocean is very stormy."

The merchants who succeeded in the maritime trade could make a fortune in a single voyage, and the ports of the Persian Gulf became great crossroads between Europe and Asia. Dubai and other Persian Gulf ports added pearls and Arabian horses to a trade that included goods from India, such as cotton, spices, and swords; products from China, such as silk, porcelain, and tea; goods from the Middle East, such as carpets, muslin, and perfumes; and goods from East Africa, such as gold and ivory.

EUROPEAN INVASIONS

As the European kingdoms grew in power, their leaders and merchants were eager to control this fantastically lucrative trade location. Portugal was one of the first to send its fleet to capture key posts in the Indian Ocean and along the coast of Africa and the Strait of Hormuz in the 1500s. One hundred years later, they were driven out by the Dutch. The British and French attempted to secure key ports in the region in the 1800s.

The British did not want to establish colonies in the Persian Gulf, but rather to control the sea routes in order to safeguard their trade with India. The Qawasim tribe, in control of Sharjah and Ra's al-Khaymah, saw the powerful British fleet as an invasion force and put up stiff resistance, frequently attacking British ships throughout the late 1700s and early 1800s. The British retaliated. They blamed the Qawasim for the piracy that was interfering with trade on the gulf. In 1819, the British attacked and burned coastal towns in the regions of Sharjah, Umm al-Qaywayn, and 'Ajmān, destroying nearly all of the ships.

Throughout history, forts have been constructed all over the world to house and protect troops at war. Today, forts often make attractive tourist destinations. The UAE is home to several forts.

One of the largest forts in the UAE is Al Jahili Fort. Built in the late 1800s, it is located in Al-'Ayn in the emirate of Abu Dhabi. It was built on the orders of the grandfather of the UAE's founder. It was built with the purpose of controlling tribes in the area but was also used as a home for the ruler's family.

Another well-known fort in the UAE is Al Bithnah. The fort is located in an area in al-Fujayrah where battles between local tribes often occurred during the 1700s. Built around 1735, this historic fort allowed locals in Al Bithnah village to protect their home.

The Al Hayl Fort, shown here, is located in al-Fujayrah. It was built around 1830.

Located just 8 miles (13 km) outside of the city of al-Fujayrah, Al Bithnah also played a role in fending off potential attacks to the city.

As the Qawasim's power declined, the tribal rulers of Abu Dhabi and Dubai rose to prominence. The al-Maktoum family set about making Dubai the leading trade center of the Gulf Coast, while Abu Dhabi emerged as the leader of the highly profitable pearling industry.

In 1835, under British pressure, the rulers of four emirates—Dubai, Abu Dhabi, 'Ajmān, and Sharjah—signed a truce outlawing acts of war at sea during the pearling season. This agreement was turned into the Perpetual Treaty of Peace in 1853. In this unusual treaty, seven emirates agreed to continue the ban on war at sea, and in return, Great Britain agreed to protect them against external attack. From this time on, the seven emirates were known as the Trucial States, and the British continued to defend them and manage their foreign affairs.

THE UAE FORMS

The British agreement with the Trucial States helped to fend off other powers, especially France, Germany, and the Ottoman Empire, which had hoped to gain influence in the Persian Gulf in the late 19th and early 20th centuries. After World War II (1939—1945), however, Great Britain declined as a world power and began to lose its colonial holdings, including India in 1947. In 1951 and 1952, the British helped establish a Trucial defense force and a council to discuss common problems faced by these states.

In 1968, Great Britain announced that it would remove its military forces from the Persian Gulf region by the end of 1971. During these same years, oil discoveries by Western oil companies were just beginning to modernize Abu Dhabi. Although the ruling family of Abu Dhabi was not prepared for the loss of British defensive support or the beginnings of great oil wealth, the sheikh was eager to create regional unity.

First, following the British announcement, Abu Dhabi and Dubai agreed to form a federation. Then, in 1970, Sheikh Zāyid ibn Sulṭān Al Nahyān, the ruler of Abu Dhabi, made the bold announcement that the oil revenues were to be "at the service of all the emirates." The Trucial States—Sharjah, 'Ajmān,

Upon the discovery of oil in 1958, the UAE's trajectory in history changed tremendously.

Umm al-Qaywayn, Ra's al-Khaymah, and al-Fujayrah—were invited to join Abu Dhabi and Dubai in the federation, as were Qatar and Bahrain.

In each emirate, a strong desire for security was tempered by an equally strong desire to maintain tribal independence. While Bahrain and Qatar declined to join, six of the emirates agreed on a federation in December 1971, with Ra's al-Khaymah holding out for two months before signing on in February 1972.

The rulers of the emirates knew that the oil discoveries made it essential for them to unite for security reasons, and world events soon confirmed their reasoning. The ambitions of the Communist Soviet Union and its invasion of Afghanistan were one cause for alarm. The Iran-Iraq War, which began in 1980, and the continuing Arab-Israeli conflict also revealed how volatile the region was and still is. In addition, Iran occupied two islands claimed by Sharjah and Ra's al-Khaymah, a dispute that has not yet been resolved as of 2021. Iraq's invasion of Kuwait in 1990 brought the danger very close to home.

These events have made it clear that the UAE and its neighboring oil-producing countries were of tremendous importance to the world. To aid in their own defense, the UAE joined with the five other oil-rich monarchies in 1981—Saudi Arabia, Kuwait, Bahrain, Qatar, and Oman—to form the Gulf Cooperation Council. They also rely on the major nations that depend on their oil, especially the United States, for protection against other countries that threaten their sovereignty. The United States, in turn, showed its commitment to the Persian Gulf states' independence in 1990 and 1991, when it rushed to the aid of Kuwait after Iraq, then led by the dictator Saddam Hussein, invaded.

THE OIL INDUSTRY BOOMS

Most of the Persian Gulf monarchies had signed agreements with consortiums, or combinations of Western oil companies, beginning in the 1930s. In 1958, following earlier discoveries of oil in Saudi Arabia and Kuwait, oil was found in Abu Dhabi. More discoveries followed, but Dubai had to wait another 10 years for its own oil to start flowing. When the offshore and land discoveries were surveyed, experts found that the UAE was perched atop about 98 billion barrels of oil, constituting about 10 percent of the world's total. Most of the oil is in Abu Dhabi, with Dubai a distant second. The other emirates have little or no oil. In the 1970s, the UAE became one of the original members of the Organization of the Petroleum Exporting Countries (OPEC).

Over the next three decades, the UAE was transformed. Poverty and hunger rates lowered significantly. Spectacular high-rise luxury hotels, office buildings, and apartment complexes popped up in what were once poorer areas. The Emirati and their leaders looked ahead, planning for the federation's future.

Since the oil industry began growing, the UAE has rapidly transformed. While lifestyles have greatly changed due to this transformation, many traditions and practices have been preserved and even expanded. The people of the country and their government have worked on and continue to work on various projects to protect the desert and coastal environment. Additionally, as the economy has grown, hundreds of thousands of newcomers from other parts of the world have entered the country for work and travel. One issue UAE society has dealt with due to this growth is how to embrace these newcomers without losing the traditional Arab customs and values that fuel so much of the nation's history. Today, the UAE is an important part of the world, for its contributions to both the oil and business industries. In this ever-expanding world, it seems safe to say the UAE's future will likely hold even more growth.

INTERNET LINKS

www.history.com/this-day-in-history/united-arab-emirates-is-formed
This article details how the United Arab Emirates were formed.

www.uae-embassy.org/about-uae/history
Read more about the nation's history on this website from the UAE Embassy in Washington, D.C.

GOVERNMENT

The flag of the United Arab Emirates is red, green, white, and black. Each color has its own meaning, and together they stand for unity.

3

WHEN THE UNITED ARAB EMIRATES officially formed in 1971, not everyone was sure it would be successful. Several kingdoms were coming together in an attempt to form a unified nation. Such an effort had not successfully occurred in recent years. While the leaders of the Trucial States had experience running their own emirates, they did not have experience running a federal government. To be successful, the nation would require a delicate balance between the national government and the emirates. Some weren't sure it was possible. Today, though, anyone who was once skeptical must admit they were wrong. The seventh emirate joined the federation in February 1972, and over the last 50 years or so, the UAE has both grown as a nation and embraced differences among the individual emirates.

"The ruler should not have any barrier which separates him from his people."
—Sheikh Zāyid ibn Sulṭān Al Nahyān

The success of the UAE relies largely on the cooperation of all the emirates. The rulers of the smaller emirates must protect their local interests while also working for the good of the country. The rulers of Abu Dhabi and Dubai have to be careful not to dominate even though, due to their size and wealth, they could exercise overwhelming power, such as by insisting that oil revenues be used only as they wished. This, however, could cause resentment and would have the potential to create unrest.

Sheikh Khalīfah became president of the UAE and leader of Abu Dhabi after his father died in 2004.

A BALANCED FEDERAL GOVERNMENT

Many Emirati are proud of their young nation, but they also feel deep loyalty toward their families, their tribes, and to the sheikh of their emirate. The importance of these loyalties is evident in many aspects of the government. According to the 1971 constitution, for example, the president and vice president are to be elected every five years by the Supreme Council. In practice, however, the president is always a member of the Al Nahyān clan of Abu Dhabi, and the vice president and prime minister is from Dubai's al-Maktūm tribe.

Sheikh Zāyid ibn Sulṭān Al Nahyān was the UAE's first president, serving from its founding until his death on November 2, 2004. His son Sheikh Khalīfah ibn Zāyid Al Nahyān was elected to replace him the next day. Similarly, Vice President Sheikh Muhammad ibn Rāshid al-Maktūm was elected by the Supreme Council in January 2006 to replace his brother.

When the federation was formed in 1971, the seven rulers agreed to turn certain functions over to the federal government. In general, the Supreme Council of Rulers, headed by the president and vice president, is responsible for the foreign affairs, security and defense, public health, education, currency, matters of nationality and immigration, and postal service and telecommunications of the country. Other functions of the federal government

The Federal Supreme Council of Rulers is made up of the rulers of all seven emirates. In addition to electing the president and vice president, the council acts as the highest constitutional authority, setting general policies for the country. The rulers meet several times a year, and they work together and vote on important measures. In practice, the rulers of Abu Dhabi and Dubai can veto any measure they disapprove of, giving these two emirates more power than the smaller emirates. However, the rulers of both Abu Dhabi and Dubai commonly try to avoid doing this and aim to have a consensus on every issue.

include air-traffic control, labor relations, issues involving territorial waters, and the extradition of criminals. All other domestic matters are left to the individual emirates.

The main executive body for carrying out these federal functions is the Council of Ministers, which operates much like a cabinet does in other countries. The Council of Ministers consists of various department heads, such as the minister of labor and the minister of education. The ministers are headed by a prime minister, appointed by the president and the Supreme Council of Rulers.

All the other ministers are similarly chosen, and they can come from any of the emirates. To ensure that the interests of all the emirates are represented, efforts are made to select at least one or two ministers from every emirate.

The UAE's legislative branch is called the Federal National Council (FNC). This is not to be confused with the Supreme Council of Rulers or the Council of Ministers. This is a one-house body made up of 40 members chosen for two-year terms by the rulers of the emirates. The 40 members are distributed to each emirate based on population. As of 2021, the FNC has eight members each from Abu Dhabi and Dubai, six each from Sharjah and Ra's al-Khaymah, and four each from al-Fujayrah, Umm al-Qaywayn, and 'Ajmān. The main function of the FNC is not to create or propose legislation, as legislative bodies do in

In addition to each of the emirates cooperating with each other effectively, the UAE as a whole must cooperate with neighboring countries. The Gulf Cooperation Council (GCC), shown here meeting in Abu Dhabi, is a union of Arab states bordering the Persian Gulf.

When the federation was formed, all seven emirates had long-established governments. All were, and still are, controlled by the ruling family and its sheikh, or emir. The sheikhs hold regular majlis within their own emirates, as they have done for many years.

The Abu Dhabi government is the largest and most complex of the local governments. An important part of it is the National Consultative Council, made up of members of the oldest families and tribes in the emirate.

The main cities also have Municipal Councils. These councils manage local matters such as traffic control, minor crimes, and sanitation.

other countries. Instead, the 40 members "review" new measures passed by the Supreme Council of Rulers. They can suggest changes but not actually make them.

The existence of the FNC gives people and ruling families in the smaller emirates a real sense of participation. The Arab name for FNC is Majlis Watani Ittihad. The word *majlis* refers to an ancient custom in which anyone can appear before a ruler to state needs, suggestions, opinions, or complaints. This has always enabled people to feel that they are involved in the government and for the ruler to hear what might be troubling his subjects.

The constitution also establishes an independent judiciary for national matters. The judges for this Union Supreme Court are appointed by the president.

THE FATHER OF THE UAE

Sheikh Zāyid ibn Sulṭān Al Nahyān was far more than the first president of the UAE. He was the founder and the driving force behind the creation of the federation. He's often called the father of the UAE. Many would say he was responsible for bringing unity to seven desert emirates. He served as president from the country's founding in 1971 until his death in 2004.

Born in 1918 in Abu Dhabi, Sheikh Zāyid spent many of his early days moving stones and planting trees to restore the ancient system of canals needed to irrigate the date palms of Abu Dhabi. In 1966, he replaced his brother Sheikh Shakhbūṭ ibn Sulṭān, who had ruled Abu Dhabi since 1928.

Sheikh Zāyid is often credited with having had great skill in establishing harmony among the seven very different emirates while working to create the federation after the British announced their withdrawal from the Persian Gulf. He built their confidence in Abu Dhabi and the federation by helping the poorer emirates financially and creating huge public works programs throughout the country.

One of Sheikh Zāyid's special projects was "greening the desert" by using desalinated water for landscaping and planting. The city of Abu Dhabi is now home to many parks and thousands of acres of grass, watered by electric sprinklers and decorated with splendid fountains. Making the desert bloom was one of Sheikh Zāyid's main goals, and keeping that part of his history alive seems to be a fitting tribute to the father of the UAE.

The year 2018 marked 100 years since Sheikh Zāyid's birth. The UAE's current leader, Sheikh Khalīfah ibn Zāyid Al Nahyān, declared it to be the "Year of Zāyid" in honor of his late father.

Sheikh Zāyid is still an important figure in the UAE. His likeness can be found around the country, such as on this poster in Abu Dhabi.

After the September 11, 2001, terrorist attacks, the United States launched a war on terrorism throughout the world. Antiterrorism agents soon discovered that two of the eleven highjackers were citizens of the UAE. They also found that some of the funds used by the terrorists had come from bank accounts in Dubai.

UAE officials worked closely with American agents to close the bank accounts and to tighten the laws governing banks in the emirates. They also supplied information about any individuals in the UAE suspected of having ties to terrorist organizations. In addition, the emirates continued to make their port and airfield facilities available to U.S. military forces. These efforts convinced most U.S. leaders that the emirates were genuine allies. According to a report released in December 2020 from the U.S. Department of State, "The United States has had friendly relations with the United Arab Emirates (UAE) since 1971."

BOUNDARY DEBATES

Because of the loyalty of people to their families, tribes, and sheikh, the boundaries between emirates were rather loosely drawn. Families that were technically living in one emirate might actually be part of a tribe in a neighboring emirate. The result is the existence of small enclaves of people who feel that they do not belong to the emirate in which they are physically located. About 10 miles (16 km) inside the border of Abu Dhabi, for example, there are small settlements of people who belong to al-Fujayrah's Sharqiyyin tribal group.

Similarly, the UAE's boundaries with Saudi Arabia and Oman have often been disputed. For example, both the United Arab Emirates and Saudi Arabia claim a strip of coastline that borders Qatar to the northwest, and at times, both Saudi Arabia and Oman have attempted to claim the oases around the city of Al-'Ayn as their own. While the countries have attempted agreements, it is still unclear where exactly the countries' borders lie.

GROWTH OF THE FNC

Before December 2006, all FNC members were appointed by their emirate's ruler. This meant that it was more than likely that the members all generally agreed with their ruler on key political topics, whether or not that reflected the opinions of the general public. However, in December 2006, the first indirect election of FNC members was held. Under the new rules, each ruler still appoints half of their emirate's FNC members, but the other half are elected by an electoral college made up of members selected by the emirate's ruler.

After the 2015 elections, almost a quarter of the FNC's members were women. The same year, Dr. Amal Al Qubaisi was elected president of the FNC, making her the first-ever female speaker of an Arab national parliament. At the end of 2018, Sheikh Khalīfah said that 50 percent of the FNC should be occupied by Emirati women. This resulted in 20 of the council's seats being held by women after the election and appointing of new members in 2019.

"Women are half of our society; they should be represented as such."

—Sheikh Muhammad ibn Rāshid al-Maktūm

INTERNET LINKS

www.bbc.com/news/world-middle-east-14703998
Learn more about the UAE, including its government, here.

constituteproject.org/constitution/United_Arab_Emirates_2009?lang=en
You can read the entire constitution of the UAE here.

globaledge.msu.edu/countries/united-arab-emirates/government
This page from Michigan State University offers an easy-to-understand overview of the UAE government.

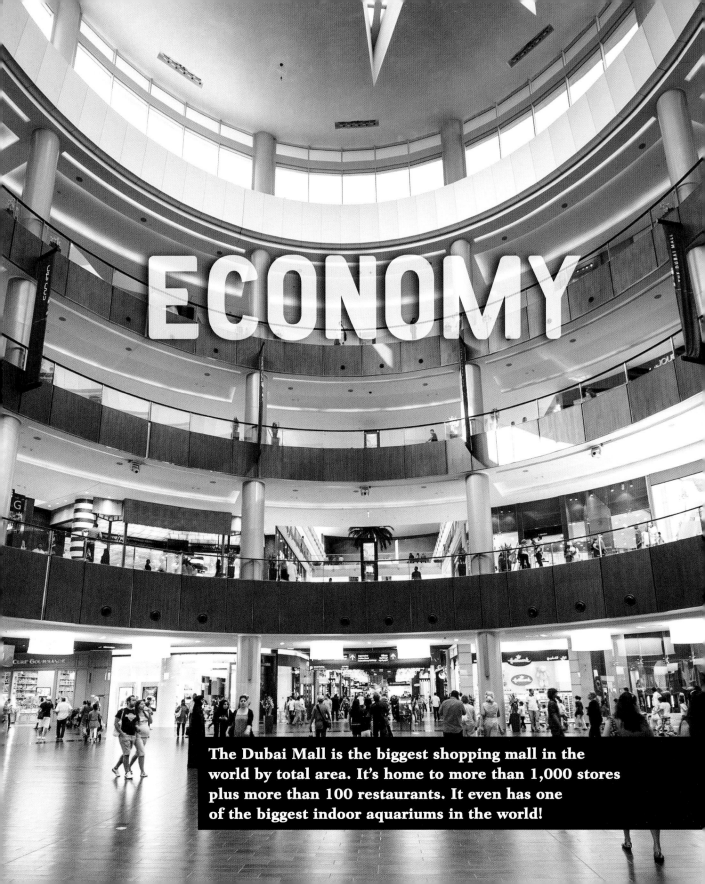

ECONOMY

The Dubai Mall is the biggest shopping mall in the world by total area. It's home to more than 1,000 stores plus more than 100 restaurants. It even has one of the biggest indoor aquariums in the world!

4

WE ALREADY KNOW OIL IS A HUGE part of the economy of the United Arab Emirates, but it's far from the only part of the economy that is thriving. Oil is a finite resource, meaning it can run out, and once it does, there won't be any more of it to use. This is just part of the reason the UAE's people and rulers are determined to build a future that does not depend solely on oil.

While oil is still lucrative, the UAE has also turned its sights on another key industry in order to diversify its economy: tourism. In particular, the big cities of the United Arab Emirates—Dubai, Abu Dhabi, and Sharjah—are popular tourist destinations. Some of the largest skyscrapers in the world, luxurious resort hotels, gorgeous beaches, parks filled with greenery and fountains, and world-class shopping malls are just some of the things tourists come home from the UAE raving about.

THE PRE-OIL ECONOMY

Before the oil boom, a large part of the population living in what is now the UAE lived in poverty. Many families struggled to make ends meet. Much of the work that was available was extremely physically demanding.

In coastal areas, mountain wadis, and oases, people relied on irrigation and wells to grow their date palms and crops. The date palm was their

RECORD-SETTING HEIGHTS

Dubai in particular is known for its soaring skyscrapers. In fact, it's home to the tallest building in the world, at least as of 2021: the Burj Khalifa. Completed in 2010, the Burj Khalifa reaches higher than 2,700 feet (823 m) and has 163 floors. As of 2021, it was still the tallest building in the world, but at least one construction project, in Saudi Arabia, was in the works, aiming

Even in Dubai, a city full of many tall buildings, the Burj Khalifa towers over its neighboring skyscrapers.

to beat the record. If this building is completed, will the UAE attempt to build an even taller building? Some people think it's possible, but only time will tell.

all-encompassing plant, used to make houses, tents, farming tools, fishing nets, and small boats.

The scarcity of water made camels the most important livestock. They were used primarily for transportation and were known as the "ships of the desert." The animals could go without water for up to two weeks in the summer, and two or three months in the winter. The fertile land around the oases, coasts, and mountains also supported goats and sheep, which were important sources of wool, meat, and milk.

Farm life was hard, but the life of the desert Bedu tribe was far harder. The Bedu, also sometimes called Bedouin, engaged in a continual search for grazing land and water for their flocks and camels. Thirst and starvation were constant dangers.

Family and tribal ties formed a web that linked the people of the inland oases to the people of the coast. Often, the men would move to the coast in the spring to spend the summer diving for pearls.

Coastal people relied on small-scale trading, pearl diving, and fishing to survive. They used an amazing array of dhows, the sizes, shapes, and construction of which were determined by their intended use. Different designs were used for fishing, pearl diving, and long-distance trade; smaller boats were used for transportation on the creeks.

Fishing provided not only food but, for families owning a boat, a source of revenue. The warm waters of the Persian Gulf support more than 700 species of fish. Usually, men went to sea to fish, and women sold what was caught. Fish were caught in nets or in cleverly designed cages known as *gargour*, which were made of palm leaves. Some of the fish were dried and stored or exported.

Pearling was a good part-time occupation, at least until the 1930s. It was a dangerous life, but it promised divers the possibility of fabulous wealth. Wearing nose clips made of turtle shells, the men dove to 100 feet (30 m) or more and stayed submerged for up to three minutes to do this difficult work.

The coastal towns were also the centers of the maritime trade. For example, even before the oil boom began, Dubai had been promoting trade between India and markets in the Middle East and Europe. In addition, market areas called *souks* were found in these towns and were divided into separate quarters according to the trade involved. Some sold food, while others specialized in spices or in handicrafts, such as pottery, wooden items, or jewelry.

While camels were incredibly important for transportation, they were also a source of milk, meat, and wool.

STRIKING OIL

The first discovery of oil in the UAE was made in Abu Dhabi in 1958. The discovery of oil in Dubai came a little later, and petroleum production began

Today, oil pumps such as these can be found in deserts around the Arabian Peninsula.

there in 1969. Today, the UAE is one of the top oil-producing countries in the world. Abu Dhabi can take credit for most of it, producing about 95 percent of the country's oil. The other meaningful supply comes from Dubai. At one point, Dubai produced as much as one-sixth of all the country's oil, but as the emirate expanded its economy into other industries, its oil production slowed. Sharjah and Ra's al-Khaymah have small pockets of oil as well, but not enough to support a major industry. Sharjah, however, also has natural gas. Once again, though, Abu Dhabi takes credit for the most natural gas fields in the federation. Altogether, the UAE has one of the largest natural gas reserves in the world.

The oil boom was given a terrific boost by changes in the world market. The UAE was one of the first of the 13 countries to join OPEC. In 1973, OPEC quadrupled the price of oil. Then, it made another huge increase in 1979, when the price of a barrel of crude oil increased from about $5 to $34.

At the time, four Gulf States—the UAE, Saudi Arabia, Kuwait, and Qatar—held 45 percent of the world's oil. European and American businesspeople rushed to the Persian Gulf to propose all sorts of construction and investment schemes. Abu Dhabi's emir and the president of the federation, Sheikh Zāyid, kept his pledge to help the poorer emirates and those with no oil. Major programs were launched in each of the emirates to develop infrastructure such as electric power, roads, airports, harbor facilities, schools, hospitals, and clinics.

MODERNIZING THE ECONOMY

By the late 1980s, the UAE had nearly completed its infrastructure. The rulers had also created the ideal welfare state. There were no taxes, and every Emirati was guaranteed an education and employment. Medical care was provided for free in well-equipped hospitals. Utilities, such as water, electricity, and oil products, were nearly free.

Today, the UAE's oil is exported to other countries. Centuries ago, another underground resource, copper, was mined and shipped to other places from what's now the UAE. Archaeological sites in the UAE and Oman show that the people of the region were mining, processing, and exporting copper as early as 3000 BCE. It is estimated that, over several centuries, thousands of tons of copper were exported. The copper trade apparently continued through the Middle Ages.

In an effort to reduce the UAE's dependence on oil revenues, copper mining has been reintroduced on a small scale. An added bonus of refining the copper has been the discovery of small pockets of gold and silver.

The rulers, and the planners they hired, worked to find ways to diversify the economy so as to become less dependent on oil. Desalination plants were built to provide water for the cities and to expand green areas. Local agriculture was promoted, resulting in a remarkable increase in agricultural output.

Other plans included developing industries, including a state-of-the-art aluminum plant. Steel, petrochemical, and concrete plants soon followed. Eventually, companies and factories were created for food processing, furniture production, and pharmaceuticals production.

Another major move was the establishment of the Jebel Ali Free Zone created by the Dubai government in 1985. In this huge area covering 38 square miles (100 sq km), Dubai provides tax-free shipping and storage facilities with the world's largest artificial port, including ready-made factories and living quarters for workers. Transportation and communications systems are up to date. In other words, a company can simply sign a lease for all the buildings and other facilities it needs and commence its manufacturing operation. Black & Decker, Honda, Mercedes-Benz, Nestle, and Sony are among the approximately 8,000 companies with locations at Jebel Ali.

One of the most exciting and visible areas of growth has been the tourism industry. The UAE's three main cities have outstanding facilities for tourists, such as several five-star hotels and restaurants, beaches and swimming pools, amusement parks, and museums. Vacationers can take trips from the cities into the desert or to oases. There are also horse races, golf courses, dhow excursions, fishing, and dolphin watching. Perhaps one of the most surprising aspects of the UAE's tourism industry is the number of wealthy people from other countries who have purchased vacation homes there.

FOREIGN WORKERS

UAE rulers and business leaders are eager to employ Emirati in executive positions, but a shortage of qualified professionals in the fields most lucrative to the nation has made that difficult. Hopefully, the education reform that has occurred in recent decades will help that to change in the future. However, as it is now, a huge number of foreign workers have been hired to fill a wide variety of jobs, from simple construction tasks to marine zoology research. Many companies in the UAE are also multinational firms, and because of this, the companies often recruit employees from other countries.

Many of the foreign workers, or expatriates, receive excellent salaries and company benefits, and that proves to be a strong enough incentive for them to leave home for months or years at a time. To attract qualified workers, some companies offer special incentives, such as paid leave once or twice a year, and sometimes a round-trip airline ticket.

There are negative aspects of being an expatriate worker. In almost all cases, for example, expatriates cannot become UAE citizens. They do not enjoy many of the benefits of citizenship, such as getting free education, health care, and electricity. More serious are the allegations that some workers are being mistreated by being forced to work long hours, for example, or to work under hazardous or unhealthy conditions. In addition, reports indicate that workers from southern and southeastern Asia work mostly in menial jobs, such as driving taxis and performing unskilled work in the petroleum industry. Many are forced into these jobs when they lose their better jobs to Emirati who have completed training.

In spite of the difficulties, many expatriates remain because either they enjoy the life or they cannot resist the wages, which tend to be generous. Some also go to the UAE to escape unrest in their home countries, such as Lebanon. Expatriates continue to make up almost 90 percent of the UAE's population.

Some expatriates have lived in the UAE since the oil boom days of the 1970s. Their children have grown up in the UAE and have gone to local schools. The result is a mixing of ethnicities and cultures, which enriches life in the UAE. Some Emirati are concerned, however, because they are a minority in their own country. They worry that their traditional values and customs may disappear.

The currency of the UAE is called the dirham.

LOOKING FORWARD

In the 1980s, there was a surplus of oil on the world market, and the prices of petroleum products dropped sharply. This jolted the economy of the UAE, as well as other oil-rich countries. The UAE found itself, like other countries of the world, building up a sizable national debt. The rulers became determined to plan more wisely in the future.

The world market soon bounced back, and oil prices returned to $34 a barrel. The market was shaken in a different way in 2005 when oil shortages developed, and by the close of the year, prices had shot to almost $70 a barrel, doubling revenues for the OPEC countries.

Instead of pouring around 80 percent of the revenues into new projects, as in the past, the UAE began using only about 40 percent to foster economic expansion. Much of the wealth was instead used to reduce its debt and to invest in safe stock and bond markets. In 2005, for example, the UAE purchased $1 billion in shares of the auto manufacturer DaimlerChrysler. Even greater amounts were invested in U.S. Treasury bonds, which help to finance America's huge debt.

While oil is still a key part of the UAE's income, creating a future less dependent on oil has become important for the nation—and the rest of the

In 2020, Dubai returned to the global financial market, in an attempt to potentially raise billions of dollars. It also let the world know that the country's debt was smaller than experts had thought.

world. Oil is a fossil fuel. It has harmful effects on the environment, and the supply we have won't last forever, especially if we keep using it at the rate we do now. The UAE depends on high-energy technologies, like water desalination and air-conditioning. Because of this, it has one of the highest per capita rates of energy consumption in the world. In order to combat these issues before they get worse, the country has started to invest in other forms of energy—renewable ones. For example, in 2013, Abu Dhabi opened a facility which, at the time, was one of the largest solar power plants in the world. The facility was capable of powering up to 20,000 homes. Then, in 2020, Abu Dhabi secured funding for a project that would double the size of the old plant. This new plant is expected to create enough electricity to provide power for about 160,000 homes in the UAE.

"We will look at the future with optimism even when the last barrel of oil leaves, because our youth, in whom we have invested, comprise our real wealth."
—Sheikh Saif bin Zayed, UAE Deputy Prime Minister and Minister of the Interior

INTERNET LINKS

www.guinnessworldrecords.com/records/hall-of-fame/burj-khalifa-tallest-building-in-the-world
Find out more about the Burj Khalifa, and watch a video about the tallest building in the world, as of 2021.

https://jafza.ae/
Learn more about the Jebel Ali Free Zone here.

ENVIRONMENT

Sandstorms are not uncommon in the UAE. People often wear masks to protect themselves from inhaling harmful particles during these storms.

5

ECOSYSTEMS IN GENERAL ARE fragile things. A seemingly small change to one part of the system can impact the rest of the system. In desert environments, this rings even more true. If one part of the system is disturbed, the entire system can often see the effects. For example, with such little water in deserts, one underground spring drying up could cause an entire plant species to die out. This could also cause animals to move away. These changes can, in turn, affect other parts of the system as well.

It is important for those living in a desert environment to work within its limits. The Emirati have, in general, lived in harmony with their environment. Traditionally, for example, farmers would make only modest changes to the environment by extending their stone-lined irrigation channels. However, as technologies have improved and industries have changed, so, too, have the ways people interact with their environment—not just in the UAE, but in the world as a whole. For example, with the UAE's influx of oil money came access to modern technology and the ability to make radical changes to the environment. In many ways, these changes made life easier, such as by speeding up work processes or making the hot desert climate more comfortable to live in. However, we now know that many newer technologies often require more energy and can have unintended negative consequences, especially when it comes to their impact on the environment. An economic shift toward renewable energy sources is just one way the leaders of the UAE are working toward keeping the environment hospitable and healthy for years to come.

ANIMAL PROTECTION

Industrializing an area or building infrastructure for oil fields can take away habitats that once belonged to animals. However, long before the drilling of oil, hunting reduced the populations of many desert mammals. Some were hunted for food, while others were hunted as trophies by large hunting parties, often organized by wealthy sheikhs. Sometimes, predator populations are purposely reduced because of a danger they pose to livestock. One example of this is the Arabian leopard. Today, these animals are classified as critically endangered, with only an estimated population of 200 remaining the wild, and far fewer remaining in the UAE.

In addition to the Arabian leopard, other endangered species include the Arabian tahr, a goatlike animal that lives high in the mountains. The tahr was thought to be extinct, but a 1995 wildlife survey found that some have survived at altitudes above 2,000 feet (600 m). The survival of the Arabian gazelle was also discovered during the same 1995 survey. The caracal, a reddish brown, nocturnal cat, seems to have survived by hunting at night and sleeping during the day. Several other mammals, including the desert wolf, Gordon's wildcat, and striped hyena, are rarely seen in the wild.

Several ruling families have been active in protecting these and other rare species. The late president Sheikh Zāyid ibn Sulṭān Al Nahyān was one of the pioneers of the country's ambitious conservation efforts. When he transformed the island off the coast of Abu Dhabi into the Sir Bani Yas Nature Reserve, he envisioned a place where endangered species could roam freely. Throughout its years of conservation efforts, the island has provided homes for and preserved many animals.

ARTIFICIAL ISLANDS

In 2001, off the shore of Dubai, work started on a project known as the Palm Islands. In an effort to increase tourism, hundreds of tons of sand were dredged up from the floor of the Persian Gulf and moved to carefully planned locations along the coast. Boulders and stones from the mainland were used too. Gradually, narrow, gracefully curved islands forming the shape of palm trees began to take shape.

The Palm Islands were originally supposed to include three separate developments: Palm Jumeirah, Palm Jebel Ali, and Palm Deira. Palm Jumeirah is the smallest of the three, but as of March 2021, it is the only one that has actually been completed. Work on Palm Jebel Ali and Palm Deira were stopped because of economic uncertainty. Still, Palm Jumeirah alone is a fascinating sight. Today, wealthy families and individuals own lavish private residences on the islands, and tourists flock to the hotels and shops of Palm Jumeirah.

Even unfinished, the Palm Islands are a unique and interesting part of the UAE. Before construction began, environmentalists had an array of questions about the ambitious project. Would erosion wear away these artificial islands? Could their proximity to the shore significantly alter the action of waves and tides along the coast? Would the region's marine life be disrupted by the huge construction project? Along with the rapid growth of the entire city of Dubai, could the coastal ecosystem support so many people?

The developers seemed relatively unconcerned, however, because they said they had analyzed most of the potential problems. As it turns out, though, the islands have indeed resulted in environmental problems. At first, marine life seemed to be thriving around the new islands, and fragile coral reefs actually expanded enough to create a new area for snorkeling. However, more than a decade after the completion of Palm Jumeirah, several problems are quite apparent. Drastic changes to the wave, temperature, and erosion patterns in the Persian Gulf occurred due to the intense dredging needed to build these islands. Additionally, at least 1 square mile (2.5 sq km) of coral was killed in the process of forming the islands. These and other potential issues need to

Near the Palm Islands off the coast of Dubai is another group of man-made islands. Like Palm Deira and Palm Jebel Ali, this project remains incomplete. Building of the World Islands began in 2003. As the name suggests, the islands were meant to resemble a map of the world when viewed from above. The completed project would have 300 small islands. This seemed like a cool plan, but the problem, once again, was erosion. Due to erosion, other weathering, and sinking, most of the islands have lost their shape. You can still tell that the islands make up the general shape of the world, but it is not quite as impressive as initially intended. As of 2016, only nine of the islands had been developed, and the islands representing the continents of Africa, Asia, Australia, and South America all remained entirely uninhabited. In 2021, it was reported that only two or three of the islands were completely functional.

This photo shows several of the World Islands that have been built on. Beyond them, you can see many more that are bare.

be explored further if the other islands are ever to be completed or future islands built.

SPECIAL PROGRAMS

The careful management of water resources is a matter of vital importance to desert nations. In the UAE, experts in water management have found that, even with the ambitious desalination programs currently in place, the country faces serious water issues. One problem involves the oases and other agricultural regions, where the overuse of irrigation has led to a buildup of salt in the soil, resulting in a sharp decline in agricultural productivity. The UAE has long been looking for ways to resolve these and other environmental issues.

While there are certainly plenty of environmental issues to be solved, as there are nearly everywhere on Earth, the UAE is working toward change.

Conferences are one way the UAE seeks ideas for how to protect the environment. An annual conference on date palms seeks to find environmentally safe ways to increase production and deal with pests that threaten date palms.

"GREENING" THE DESERT

The late president Sheikh Zāyid was devoted to the dream of "greening" the desert, and he made use of Abu Dhabi's oil revenues to advance that dream. The use of desalinated water from the Persian Gulf made the project feasible. Citizens and homeowners are often given opportunities to get trees and outdoor plants at no cost besides what it costs to plant and care for them.

The president's program led to the creation of more than 20 parks in the city of Abu Dhabi and around 3,700 acres (1,500 hectares) of grass. Other parts of the country also house many parks, often with pools or fountains. The added greenery has helped to ease the oppressive summer heat and has made the cities more pleasant for visitors. An unexpected benefit has been an increase in birdlife.

Parks often make great homes for birds that might otherwise not do well in the desert.

One initiative taken on by Abu Dhabi is known as the Masdar Initiative. Launched in April 2006, this is a multibillion-dollar investment in renewable and alternative energy and clean technology. *Masdar* means "source" in Arabic. One of its main goals is to find and utilize energy sources that will support the environment for the future. In 2018, the initiative broke ground on Masdar City, aiming for it to be one of the most sustainable cities in the world. Everything about Masdar City is meant to encourage a greener future. For example, it prioritizes pedestrians over motor vehicles. Additionally, the Masdar Green Real Estate Investment Trust (EIT) is the first EIT in the UAE to invest only in sustainable real estate properties.

INTERNET LINKS

www.atlasobscura.com/places/world-islands
Check out this article for more facts about the World Islands.

www.ead.gov.ae/en
Go to the official website of Abu Dhabi's Environmental Agency to learn more about what the emirate is doing to help the environment.

masdarcity.ae/en
Learn all about Masdar City here.

EMIRATI

Dubai is the most populous city in the UAE. As of 2021, it had a population of more than 3 million people.

6

P EOPLE MOVE TO THE UNITED ARAB Emirates from all over the world. Today, the population is not only extremely diverse, it is also growing at an extremely quick rate. Estimates put the population of the UAE at about 277,000 when the federation was formed in 1971. By 2000, that number had surpassed 3 million. In early 2021, the population was approaching 10 million.

At less than 12 percent of the population, UAE citizens are a minority of the residents in the United Arab Emirates.

Still, Emiratis only make up a small percentage of their country's population. In spite of the rapid change and growth, however, visitors are struck by the friendliness of the people and the absence of serious tension between the various ethnic groups. Two customs, developed over many centuries, help to explain this openness and tolerance. First, in desert Arab cultures, hospitality is a basic rule of survival. A Bedu herdsman, miles from any oasis, on seeing strangers approach, will automatically start preparing coffee and rush out to greet them. This custom of hospitality is still important in modern life. Although today's city dwellers are more reserved, they are still willing to drop everything to help someone in need. The second custom, openness to people from other cultures, emerges from the long history of seafaring and coastal trade in the region. This has helped to make coastal people in the UAE open to new ideas and new people.

Balancing these customs with pragmatism is a wise business practice. The merchants and businesspeople of the UAE have a reputation for being tough bargainers. Whether in an elegant steel and glass business tower or in a rug merchant's souk, many will haggle over prices until they are satisfied that the deal is fair.

PEOPLE FROM ALL OVER

In addition to identifying with their national identity as Emiratis, many people native to the UAE identify even more closely with the tribes their family comes

In the big cities of the UAE, tourists, expatriates, and Emiratis can all be seen enjoying the same restaurants or shopping in the same shops.

from. Many of these tribes date back thousands of years, well before the UAE came together as a federation.

With such a small population of Emiratis, that means there is a large population of expatriates. These people come from all parts of the world and are drawn to the emirates primarily by job and business opportunities. The expatriate population is made up mainly of people from South Asian countries. Many people come to the UAE from India and the Philippines. Additionally, a large part of the population is made up of people from Arab countries outside the UAE, as well as Iran. A much smaller portion of the country's population comes from other countries, including those in Europe and North America.

INEQUALITY AT WORK

Although there are no visible signs of ethnic tension, many human rights groups are concerned about the treatment of expatriate workers, especially the great numbers from Asian countries. These organizations report that wages are based on nationality rather than on job qualifications. There are also reports of discrimination against women and older workers.

In the uncertain life of the desert, the concept of hospitality became very complex. When a guest was welcomed to a Bedu tent, for example, he was guaranteed food, shelter, and protection for three and one-third days. This was part of a strict code of honor called sharaf. The idea of the three-plus days was that, after sharing a meal, the visitor might stay for three days, until all traces of the food had passed through his body. This was known as the bond of salt. If a visitor carried nothing but the host's salt in his system, he would still be under the host's protection.

This code of honor is of great significance to the desert Arab peoples. This code is upheld by the entire family, and it applies to all aspects of life. The Bedu (and other Arab peoples) see it as a form of protection of individual and tribal honor.

This Bedu man is pouring a cup of tea. This is a common beverage for the Bedu to offer to their guests.

Some international agencies and governments have called on the UAE to expand on workers' rights. For example, as of 2020, trade unions were not allowed in the UAE. A trade union is an organized group of workers in a certain profession or trade. Unions form to protect and further the rights and interests of workers. Unions help guarantee certain rights and benefits to workers that can otherwise be difficult to secure. Additionally, it is currently illegal for workers in the UAE to go on strike. A strike is when a group of workers refuse to work, usually because they are unsatisfied with something. In countries where striking is legal, strikes are often used as a means to improve wages or working conditions. According to UAE labor laws, employees found to be on strike can be terminated by their employers.

DESERT SURVIVAL

Although the UAE is a relatively new nation, the shared heritage of the people has helped to bind them to a shared identity. Islam and the Arab identity of the people are part of that heritage and so is their connection to the desert.

Arab tribes moved into the deserts of today's UAE more than 2,500 years ago. Most settled into permanent communities, some in coastal towns and others in the oases and other inland fertile areas, where they lived by farming and raising some livestock. Somewhat smaller numbers were the Bedu, "dwellers of the desert" in Arabic, who maintained their nomadic lifestyle, permanently engaged in a hard struggle for survival.

Today, most UAE nationals live in coastal cities and towns. Through family and tribal ties, however, urbanized families maintain close connections with those living inland, including the Bedu. Many Arabs feel a sense of identity with the Bedu. They maintain a romanticized image of the rugged and independent nomads in a way that is not unlike many Americans' feelings for the heroes of the "Wild West". Over hundreds of years, stories of the desert culture were handed down orally, and the Bedu became the heroes of many stories, poems, and songs.

Although most people in the UAE now live on the coasts, there are still those who live inland in deserts. Desert housing has evolved over the years. It once included traditional tents that protected people from the harsh winds and gusts of sand and more ventilated structures made with coral, mud, and clay. In the early 20th century, people began building wind towers on their desert homes. Called *barajils*, these towers redirected the wind in a way that allowed it to be recirculated and cool the home. If water was added to the bottom of the tower, it could make the house feel even cooler. Today, even more elaborate desert homes have courtyards in the middle to help with air circulation and high walls to keep out hot sunlight. Also, thanks to modern technology, many come with air-conditioning.

INTERNET LINKS

www.cia.gov/the-world-factbook/countries/united-arab-emirates/#people-and-society
Find up-to-date information on the people and population of the UAE.

data.worldbank.org/indicator/SP.POP.TOTL?locations=AE
View a chart of the population growth of the UAE and look at how other populations around the world have changed in recent years.

LIFESTYLE

Family time is an important part of life in the UAE.

7

AT THIS POINT, IT'S PROBABLY NOT A surprise to learn that life for nearly everyone in the UAE changed dramatically when the country began to accumulate oil wealth. Before the 1970s, life for many people in the UAE was a struggle that included poverty, hunger, and in some cases even starvation. Running water and electricity were hard to find. Health care was almost nonexistent. It was not uncommon for a woman to die during childbirth.

However, that reality has changed greatly since oil wealth found its way to the UAE. It's difficult to find a country where more has changed in recent decades when it comes to the citizens' lifestyles than the United Arab Emirates. The UAE is now the ultimate modern welfare state. Every citizen is guaranteed an education and a job, or at least an income if no job is available. There is no income tax, and health care is excellent and free. Life expectancy has increased from about 47 years in 1970 to 78 years in 2021.

In spite of the remarkable changes, important elements of the traditional lifestyle remain. The Islamic faith and loyalty to family, clan, and tribe remain the bedrock on which the social structure rests. Other

This court building sits right along the water in Sharjah.

constants, such as honor, friendliness, and generosity, continue to be evident in the daily lives of the people.

LIFE IN THE CITY

In his book *Arabian Sands*, the English explorer Sir Wilfred Thesiger wrote about his first glimpse of the town of Sharjah in the 1950s, just before the discovery of oil. "We approached a small Arab town on an open beach," he wrote. "It was as drab and tumble-down as Abu Dhabi, but infinitely more squalid, for it was littered with discarded rubbish."

Today, more than 50 years later, Sharjah is a modern city with tree-lined avenues, elegant hotels, and beautiful parks with fountains and ponds. It is also the oldest of the UAE's three major cities (the others being Dubai and Abu

Dhabi), and dozens of ancient buildings have been carefully restored, creating a pleasing mixture of the old and the new.

The seven capital cities of the emirates are all on the coast. Abu Dhabi, the nation's capital, is on an island. Dubai, Sharjah, and Ra's al-Khaymah are situated on coastal creeks. 'Ajmān, Umm al-Qaywayn, and al-Fujayrah are on sand spits wrapped around lagoons. Roughly 85 percent of the people live in these urban areas, with the majority in Dubai and Abu Dhabi.

The three largest cities are all strikingly modern. Their skylines include rows of concrete towers sporting facades of white stone and blue-green glass. To a great extent, Dubai, Abu Dhabi, and Sharjah have been built as magnets for tourists. This is especially true of Dubai, by far the largest and most extravagant city. This, after all, is the city with palm tree—shaped islands and an archipelago shaped like the world. When it comes to building things in Dubai, small is not an option. In addition to the world's tallest building, it is also home to the world's tallest hotel and the world's largest fountain. It also has one of the world's largest aquariums, an indoor ski slope (with real snow), and several large amusement parks.

Dubai has long been the commercial hub of the country, and the pace of life here is faster than that of other cities. There is a very active night life, and alcohol is allowed in many hotels and nightclubs, which is unusual in strict Muslim countries.

Abu Dhabi, the capital, seems somewhat slower paced and some might say more dignified, possibly because it is the capital. It is also the center of the oil businesses and has many ultramodern office complexes.

Sharjah, located only about 20 minutes from Dubai, is considerably smaller than the other two cities and has more reminders of its antiquity. There are traditional bazaars and souks, as well as ancient mosques, watchtowers, and forts.

The daily life in all three cities reveals the UAE's diversity. One might see Iranian rug merchants sharing coffee in a side-street souk, while Pakistani women stroll the waterfront, some with baby carriages. As afternoon shadows lengthen, Filipino and Sri Lankan boys gather for a soccer game in a city park, and nearby, Russian tourists snap photos in front of a beautiful fountain in

While Dubai is the UAE city most known for its tall skyscrapers, Abu Dhabi *(above)* has many of its own too. Architects of the UAE are also known for creating uniquely shaped buildings.

Abu Dhabi that spouts water more than 300 feet (122 m) in the air. At an outdoor café, Saudi men discuss a business deal, and several Emirati women prepare for a meeting.

Many people live in high-rise apartment buildings or in modern homes on tree-lined streets on the outskirts of the cities. Much of the business takes place in the new office towers, and shoppers head for the elegant, air-conditioned malls, where every brand name in the world can be found, alongside shops selling original creations.

Despite so much that is new, a good deal of business and buying still takes place in the souks, many of them ancient. There, among the flowing, soft colors of Indian silks, people sip strong coffee while haggling over the price of perfumes, carpets, or gold jewelry. Bargaining and the drinking of coffee are integral parts of shopping or closing business deals.

THE IMPORTANCE OF COFFEE

Coffee or tea offered to any visitor is a symbol of hospitality. The traditional coffee is called kahwa *and is made from green coffee beans. It is very strong and can be flavored with cardamom or saffron.*

Coffee is served from a traditional pot and poured into small cups without handles. Having three cups of coffee is considered polite, and when the guest has had enough, they shake the cup from side to side to indicate satisfaction.

This social custom of drinking coffee is also important in business. It is a way of cementing relationships, either socially or professionally.

TRADITIONAL WAYS OF LIFE

Although only about 15 percent of the people still live in oases and other rural areas, the rural way of life is imprinted in the minds of the Emirati. Such values as generosity, honor, and hospitality emerged from surviving in a harsh desert environment. Some traditions, however, including those involving the family, are feeling the pressure of the changing modern culture.

For example, women in the UAE have more freedom than those in most Arab Muslim countries. Many women are educated and are free to drive cars, take jobs outside the home, and even operate businesses. Many marriages are still arranged, although some reports say that this tradition has begun to fade. Marriage ceremonies continue to be festive affairs, with the two families making the arrangements, including the gift of money and jewelry given to the bride and her family.

On the traditional wedding day, the bride's house is decorated with dozens of tiny lights strung from trees and walls. Huge, colorful tents are set up, and tables are crowded with trays of food. The bride traditionally is kept in seclusion for three days prior to the wedding, and she is pampered by family, friends, and a beautician while she wears a traditional green gown and gold jewelry.

Entertainment is a large part of the celebration. This often takes place in a city hotel, with a professional singer and band. Dancing is also important, especially in rural celebrations. Dancing often includes the *ayala*, or hair dance, in which girls swing their long hair as they twirl in circles for hours, accompanied by rhythmic clapping.

TRADITIONAL HOMES

In the past, houses were commonly made with wood frames and walls and room dividers made from date palm fronds. Stone houses were built by wealthier families. The traditional barasti house had no windows because of the importance of privacy. Instead, each house had a square wind tower. Often made of stone or palm leaves, the tower was open on four sides to catch any breeze and funnel it into the rooms below.

In a typical barasti house, the front room was the public room, and the bedroom was in the rear. Social visits were an important part of daily life and still are. Men and women often socialize separately, with the men in the public part of the house and the women in the family rooms.

The barasti house has almost completely disappeared, replaced by more modern homes, but many of the traditional social patterns continue with little change. It is still customary to remove one's shoes when entering a house, for example. Food is still an essential element of every visit, with coffee or tea offered as symbols of hospitality. Dates are also frequently served, usually in a preserve called *seh*. When women gather, they may sample perfumes and then burn incense to cleanse the air.

TRADITIONAL CLOTHING

The traditional dress for women is the *aba*, also called a *shaili* or *abaya*—a black overgarment and head covering. Under the aba, women wear a loose *sirwal*, or pants, and a *kandura*—a dress often embroidered in gold or silver. Emirati women also traditionally wear a garment covering the nose and mouth called a burka. Many women who originally came from Pakistan, Bangladesh, Sri Lanka, and India wear similar overgarments. In the northern emirates, it is common for women to wear brighter, multicolored overgarments.

Men traditionally dress in a full-length robe or shirt called a *dishdash*. The head cloth, or *gutra*, is usually red checked or plain. The black rope wrapped around the head cloth is called the *agal*, and under the headdress, they wear a *kufi*—a small skullcap. Over the dishdash, men sometimes wear a cloak, called a *bisht*, which is usually black.

This photo shows people in the city of Dubai. You can see some are wearing more traditional clothing, such as the dishdash and gutra. Others are wearing jeans.

EVOLUTION OF EDUCATION

Before the early 1900s, only boys in what's now the UAE received a formal education. The traditional school—*al-Katateeb*—offered morning and afternoon sessions on learning to recite passages from the Quran. A new kind of school,

Sheikha Fatima bint Mubarak is one of the most vocal supporters of women's rights in the UAE. She is also the widow of Sheikh Zāyid, the former ruler of Abu Dhabi and the founder of the UAE. Her Highness has long believed that education is the key for allowing women to become important contributors to the nation. In 1973, she sponsored the first women's association in the UAE, the Abu Dhabi Women's Development Association. This encouraged similar groups to form in other emirates. In 1975, the General Union was established, and Sheikha Fatima became its first chairperson.

Sheikha Fatima has continually worked to empower women in all fields, from athletics and education to finance and politics.

still only for boys, was introduced in 1912. These new schools offered training in trade skills and some courses in science. The first schools for girls were opened in 1959.

Education has now become very important in the modern nation for children of all genders. Education is free and compulsory for children ages 6 to 15. Emirati are encouraged to continue their education and earn advanced degrees, especially in fields such as business, science and technology, and petroleum science. Government and business leaders are trying to move nationals into positions that are now commonly held by trained personnel from outside the UAE. Universities within the UAE include the Higher Colleges of Technology, the Petroleum Institute in Abu Dhabi, and the University of Sharjah. In addition, American University has branches in Dubai and Sharjah, and the British University is located in Dubai.

WORK LIFE

Working in the big cities of the UAE can be quite appealing to people both from the UAE and from outside of the country. However, it's important for those coming from other countries to understand that life, even in modern UAE cities like Dubai, might be quite different than what they're used to. As is the case in much of the rest of the world, many people work long hours and often put in seven days a week at work. Labor laws provide certain protections for workers, but as discussed earlier, they do not allow for unions or strikes. Additionally, it is often difficult for a worker to do anything about it if their employer breaks the labor laws.

Life in general in the UAE tends to be more conservative than in places such as the United States or Great Britain. Conservative dress codes are in place in most offices, as well as in most public spaces. Drinking alcohol is also not allowed in many public places. In general, traditional values are something to be respected and followed in the UAE.

"The UAE women are now well-positioned to assume a larger role in the sustainable development process. Their efforts, their contributions and their successes in taking the lead are evident."
—Sheikha Fatima bint Mubarak

INTERNET LINKS

motherofthenation.ae/en/mother-of-nation/biography
This page offers a detailed biography on Sheikha Fatima bint Mubarak.

www.pbs.org/lawrenceofarabia/revolt/clothing.html
Learn more about the Bedu people and their clothing here.

RELIGION

In Islam, everyone faces the same direction when praying, toward the holy city of Mecca.

8

SLAM IS NOT ONLY THE MAJORITY religion in the UAE, it is part of everyday life—even for those who are not Muslim. From most places in the major UAE cities and many places all around the UAE, you can hear the Muslim call to prayer five times a day. Salat is the daily ritual prayer for Muslims. It is said five times a day and is one of the Five Pillars of Islam, which are the five duties every Muslim is called to perform. This call to prayer is called the *adhan*. It is given from a tower, or minaret, near one of the many mosques. Adhan is called by a person known as a muezzin.

Upon hearing the muezzin's call, the faithful enter a mosque if they can, take off their shoes, and kneel, facing the holy city of Mecca. Even out in the desert, far from any minaret or mosque, a Bedu herder will still pause five times a day to express his faith by removing a small prayer rug from his pack and kneeling on it in the sand.

Roughly three-fifths of the UAE population is Muslim. The remaining two-fifths is made up of Christians, Hindus, and small numbers of Buddhists and other religious populations. While conditions differ from one emirate to another, visitors say that the UAE offers more religious freedom than

other Gulf states, including Saudi Arabia and Qatar. There are several Christian churches and schools, primarily in Dubai and Abu Dhabi.

FOLLOWERS OF ISLAM

Among the common forces that unite the people of the UAE are their Arab culture, including loyalty to family and tribe, and their Muslim religion. The religion of Islam emerged through a series of revelations experienced by the Prophet Muhammad between 610 CE and his death in 632. It is a monotheistic religion (belief in one god), and Allah is the name for their one god.

The word "Islam" means "submission" to the will of Allah. This submission involves all aspects of life. It includes rules for a person's daily conduct and social relationships. These rules for living emerge from the holy book of Islam,

the Quran, which Muslims believe contains the word of Allah as revealed to the Prophet Muhammad.

Islam has some beliefs that are similar to Judaism and Christianity, including the acceptance of Old Testament prophets, such as Abraham and Moses. Jesus Christ is also thought of as a prophet, but Muhammad is seen as the last prophet and the one to whom Allah revealed his complete message.

Muslims throughout the world are united by their adherence to the Five Articles of Islamic Faith and the practice of the Five Pillars of Islam. The Five Articles of Faith include belief in one god, angels, the revealed books, the prophets, and the Day of Judgment.

The Five Pillars of Islam are public acts of faith. Practicing them is a way of making Muslims known to one another. This creates a feeling of unity among the faithful. The public acts of faith include reciting the profession of faith;

This photo shows the largest mosque in the United Arab Emirates, the Sheikh Zayed Grand Mosque.

answering the five daily calls to collective public prayer; paying the *zakat*, or purification tax to aid the poor; fasting during the daylight hours during the holy month of Ramadan; and making the pilgrimage (or hajj) to Mecca at least once in a person's lifetime, unless prevented by health or finances.

THE HOLY MONTH

The month of Ramadan is the most solemn period in the Islamic year, the time during which Muhammad received the words found in the Quran. Ramadan is the ninth month of the Muslim calendar, which means that the exact period of 30 days differs by a few days each year.

During Ramadan, Muslims show their obedience to the will of Allah by observing a strict fast during daylight hours. Part of the day is spent in prayer, sometimes in a mosque, sometimes with family. At night, Muslims break the fast, usually with family members. The meal can extend far into the night and is interspersed with prayer.

Iftar is the evening meal with which Muslims break their fast each day during Ramadan. People often gather in large groups for Iftar.

There are two major branches of Islam: Sunni and Shia. Emirati have traditionally belonged to the Sunni Muslim branch of Islam, which is also practiced in neighboring Saudi Arabia. Today, roughly four-fifths of the Muslims in the UAE are Sunnis. The Shia sect was formed around Ali ibn Abi Talib, the fourth caliph (a descendant of Muhammad and religious leader of Islam), who was murdered in what is now Iraq. One difference between the two sects is that Sunnis make decisions based on consensus, while Shiites believe that the descendants of Ali, such as the Ayatollah of Iran, are the final authorities in spiritual matters.

ISLAM IN THE UAE TODAY

Following the discovery of oil and the formation of the federation, the influx of foreigners made the UAE a much larger society—and a multicultural one. The many centuries of exposure to foreigners and different ideas has generally made Emiratis tolerant of differences.

One way this tolerance has been displayed is in the willingness to change laws to meet the needs of a pluralistic population. For hundreds of years, the emirates had relied on Islamic law in judging both civil and criminal matters. During the late 1900s, new laws were formulated to deal with civil and commercial practices that do not rely solely on the rules and punishments laid down by Islamic law, which is also known as sharia law. However, some of the laws are still based on sharia law, and for some issues, such as divorce or child custody, even non-Muslims living in the UAE can still face sharia courts. However, many crimes are now dealt with through newer civil and criminal codes.

CHRISTIANITY IN THE UAE

Although Islam is by far the most prominent religion in the UAE, other religions have grown, especially in recent years. Hindu temples, Christian churches, and other places of worship are respected, with the understanding that no

SHARIA LAW

Sharia law, which is also known as Islamic law, was established by the caliphs who succeeded Muhammad. This body of laws is based on the Quran and the Hadith, a collection of sayings attributed to the Prophet.

The laws deal with every aspect of life and establish rules for behavior; they include penalties for certain criminal acts and for some civil interactions as well. Some penalties, such as stoning (for adultery) and amputation (for theft), could be carried out only with the approval of the ruler of the emirate in which the crime occurred.

attempt will be made by adherents of these religions to convert others. There are several Christian churches in Abu Dhabi, and Dubai has two large churches: St. Mary's, which is Roman Catholic, and the interdenominational Holy Trinity Church. There is also at least one Roman Catholic church in Sharjah.

The Christian churches follow the same practices as churches in Europe and North America. Some holidays, such as Easter, are based on the lunar calendar, so they fall on different dates every year. Other special days follow the Gregorian calendar, including Christmas (December 25) and New Year's Day (January 1).

HINDU FAITH

A significant portion of those living in the UAE who are not followers of Islam are members of the Hindu faith. Many of these people are expatriates from India, Pakistan, Sri Lanka, and other South Asian countries. There are many different Hindu sects; all are built around a series of texts, written in Sanskrit, in particular the *Bhagavad Gita* ("Song of the Lord"). Central to all the Hindu sects is the belief in an eternal force lying within all beings—an all-embracing reality called Brahma.

The final goal of worship is said to be a coming together of the individual self and the eternal. Related to this concept is the idea of the passing of an individual soul from one life form to another, also known as reincarnation. A related principle is karma, whereby one's actions bring either good or bad results, either in this life or in a reincarnation. The endless cycle of rebirth keeps the soul trapped until the individual breaks the cycle through one of several paths, such as intense devotion to the faith or ritual observance.

Followers of Hindu sects usually build small shrines in their homes in addition to a village or community temple. A divine presence is treated as an honored guest who is invited to look with kindness upon the worship ritual, which consists of carrying an image around the temple, as well as various other actions. Gifts consisting of fruit, flowers, and perfumes are offered in most sects. The purpose of the rites is for individual worshippers to identify with the divine presence.

In Hinduism, the worship ritual is called *puja*.

RELIGIOUS FREEDOM

Islam is the official religion of the United Arab Emirates. However, the country's constitution guarantees freedom of worship so long as it does not clash with public policy or morals. Religious discrimination is prohibited by law, and the constitution states that all people are equal before the law, no matter what their religious beliefs are. What is illegal, however, is for a non-Muslim person to try to convert a Muslim to a different religion or away from Islam. Blasphemy is also illegal.

INTERNET LINKS

www.bbc.co.uk/bitesize/topics/zpdtsbk/articles/zrxxgwx
Learn more about the religion of Islam here.

www.softschools.com/facts/religion/christianity_facts/993/
Read all about Christianity on this website.

www.theschoolrun.com/homework-help/hinduism
Find out more about Hinduism on this page.

LANGUAGE

Modern Standard Arabic is sometimes also called al-Fusha, classical Arabic, or literary Arabic.

9

MOST NATIVE EMIRATIS SPEAK A dialect of Gulf Arabic. Because the majority of the people living in the United Arab Emirates are not native Emiratis, however, Gulf Arabic is not universally known around the emirates. However, the dialect the Emiratis speak is very similar to dialects spoken in nearby countries. Modern Standard Arabic is taught to students in schools. Although the Arabic dialects can be quite different, there are also similarities, and people who live in areas where many dialects are spoken often learn to understand the other dialects. Even for those who have not formally learned Arabic, most people pick up enough of the language from signs, the media, and daily business to get by.

English is another commonly spoken language in the UAE, especially in the three major cities. Some schools even teach English to students as

A number of Arabic words are also used as parts of names. For example, abu *(father)* and umm *(mother) are frequently found in names, as are* ibn *or* bin *(son),* bint *(daughter), and* abd *(servant).*

The name of the founder of the federation, H H Sheikh Zāyid ibn Sulṭān Al Nahyān, shows that he was the son of Sulṭān Al Nahyān. The H H stands for "His Highness." You can tell by the name of Sheikh Zāyid's wife, Sheikha Fatima bint Mubarak, that she is a daughter of Sheikh Mubarak. Mubarak *also means "holy" or "blessed."*

a second language. Another sizable portion of the population speaks Hindi, the major language of India. Persian, the language of Iran, and Urdu, a language from India and Pakistan, are also common.

MIND YOUR MANNERS

Communication does not always involve words, of course. Various forms of nonverbal communication, such as actions, gestures, or facial expressions, can be remarkably effective in conveying meaning. Gestures or other nonverbal messages that are acceptable in one culture might be read as an insult in another. Most people in the UAE, because of their long exposure to other peoples and cultures, are relaxed about mistakes in nonverbal communication, but in spite of this friendly attitude, there are a few forms of this silent language to be aware of. For example, allowing a host to see the bottom of your feet is considered rude. The feet are the lowest part of the body. Since they touch the ground, they are also considered the dirtiest part of the body, and showing the bottom of the feet to others is a sign of disrespect. A similar example of poor form is crossing one leg over the other. Pointing with one's feet, for example when selecting an item to buy, is also a sign of rudeness.

People take off their shoes when entering a mosque. It is also good manners in the UAE to take off your shoes when entering someone's home. Even if the

ARABIC PRONUNCIATION

Different travel and language guides offer various guides for pronouncing letters in Arabic. The following samples are found in several guides.

Pronounce:

a *as in* look (oo)

ai *as in* eye

ay *as in* may

dh *as in* the

gh *as in a rolling* r

i *as in* see (ee)

kh *as in* loch *(Scottish)*

Double consonants are pronounced twice as long.

host says that it is not necessary to remove shoes, the gesture will generally be appreciated.

Visitors should always accept coffee, tea, or other light refreshments when offered. This is a traditional sign of hospitality or friendship in Bedu culture, and rejecting the offer could be considered an insult. Even taking one or two sips may be considered satisfactory and is certainly better than rejecting the offer altogether.

Travel consultants also suggest that visitors to the UAE avoid praising others based on their personal possessions. According to the Arab saying *baiti baitak*—"My house is your house"—the host is likely to feel obligated to give the item as a gift. This can also place an obligation on the guest to give a gift of comparable value at some future time.

Of course, visitors are also advised to be respectful of Muslim customs. During the holy month of Ramadan, for example, Muslims must refrain from eating or drinking during daylight hours. Out of respect for this practice, visitors who are not Muslim should avoid dining in public during the same time.

Just as with other languages, learning to write in Arabic can be difficult and students start to learn it while they are young.

WRITING IN ARABIC

Arabic is a fascinating language that seems particularly difficult for Westerners to master. The written language is unusual in several ways. One feature that is different from many written languages in Europe, the Americas, parts of Africa, and parts of Asia is that it is written across the page from right to left.

Another interesting feature of written Arabic is that the consonants are written on the line, while vowels are added as marks written above or below the line. The alphabet consists of 28 letters. All the letters are consonants except for *a*, *w* (used for a *w* or *u* sound), and *y* (used for *y* or *i* sounds). The short vowels are added by marks above or below the consonants.

LEARN SOME WORDS AND PHRASES

Hello or Welcome . . . . .Márhaba *or* ahlan

[Reply to hello] . . . . .Áhlayn

Good morning . . . . .Sabáh al-kháyr

[Reply to good morning] . . . . .Sabáh an-núr

. . . .*(may you have a morning of light)*

How are you? . . . . .Kâyf hálak *(to a man)*

. . . . .Kâyf hálik *(to a woman)*

Fine, thank you. . . . . .Zayn, al-hámdu, lillah

Please. . . . . .Min fádlak *(to a man)*

. . . . .Min fádlik *(to a woman)*

Yes . . . . .Náam *or* áiwa

No . . . . .La

Excuse me . . . . .Samáhli

My name is . . . . .Esmi

What is your name? . . . . . . .Shú ismak *(to a man)*

. . . . .Shú ismik *(woman)*

I am from the United States. . . . .Ána min Amerika

In printed Arabic, such as in a newspaper, the short vowels are often left out. However, in important documents, such as the Quran, these short vowels are not left out. In a newspaper, the name Muhammad would therefore appear in print as m-h-m-d, but written in Arabic characters of course. You would need to know the vowels that were not written in order to understand and figure out the pronunciation. This can make it difficult to translate Arabic into the Roman alphabet. Creating a pronunciation guide is also difficult. The samples used in this book are common to current travel guides.

COMMON PHRASES

Visitors to the emirates are struck by how often they hear or repeat the standard greeting:

*As-salám alaykum/*Peace be with you

*Waláykum as-salám/*And to you peace (reply)

Another common expression is *Insh'Allah*, which means "by the will of Allah (or God)." Visiting businesspeople sometimes find this irritating because they think it sounds evasive. If you were planning a meeting or conference, for example, and your Arab contacts frequently responded to a suggestion by saying *Insh'Allah*, you might wonder if they were trying to put you off. This, however, is not the intention. The frequent use of the term reflects Muslim traditions, as do many aspects of the Arabic language. Not saying the phrase might suggest that the person feels he or she has control over the future when, in fact, according to Muslim beliefs, it actually will be whatever God decides.

This man is reading an Arabic newspaper. It's likely that the short vowels are left out.

ARABIC SCRIPT

The Arabic alphabet is the second most commonly used alphabet in the world, after the Roman alphabet, which is also called the Latin alphabet. The Arabic alphabet was likely developed sometime around the 4th century CE. Each letter looks much different from those in the Roman alphabet, and in general, the characters are more curved and flowy. It might seem difficult for a person used to the Roman alphabet to learn to read Arabic, but signs are one way that non-Arabic speakers in the UAE learn to do this.

To help people from all over, stop signs are commonly shaped the same way in many countries. This stop sign shows the word "stop" in both English and Arabic.

INTERNET LINKS

www.arabacademy.com/learning-and-writing-the-arabic-alphabet/
This website offers an overview of the Arabic alphabet and offers techniques on how to best write the letters.

www.lonelyplanet.com/middle-east/narratives/practical-information/directory/etiquette
This article offers an overview of etiquette practices in the Middle East.

mena-languages.northwestern.edu/language-learning/languages-with-different-scripts/arabic-alphabet.html
Read more about the Arabic alphabet here.

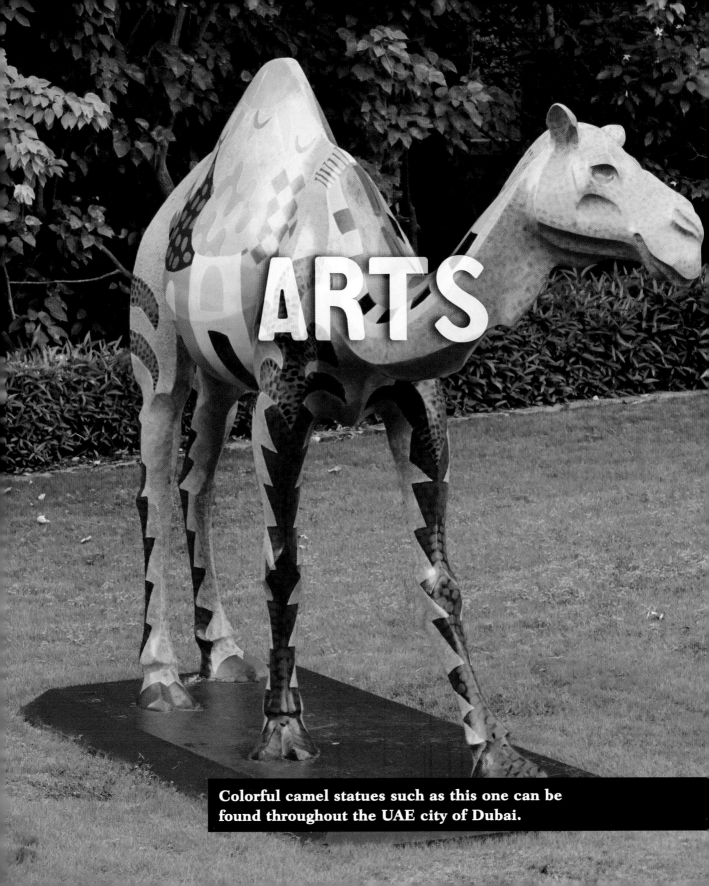

ARTS

Colorful camel statues such as this one can be
found throughout the UAE city of Dubai.

10

ART HAS LONG BEEN AN IMPORTANT part of the cultures in the part of the world we now know as the United Arab Emirates. However, life could be difficult for early inhabitants, and there was often much work to be done. This didn't leave much time for creating art—unless it also had a practical purpose. For example, some dhows were decorated with elaborate carvings. These boats were, of course, primarily a mode of transportation, but adding the carvings was a way to incorporate art and beauty into everyday necessities. Other important and necessary objects, such as weapons, tools, pottery, wind towers, and other crafted items, often displayed the skill and artistry of the craftworker, too, but the primary concern was always their function.

Yet, there has also always been a strong impulse for people to create something beautiful for its own sake. People from around the UAE have

Many people believe that the impulse to create art is part of the human experience. People have been doing it, in some form or another, for as long as they have been on Earth.

shown their artistic abilities and drive in ways such as jewelry-making and in the art of henna. Souks have long been a place for people to showcase and sell their art.

Since the United Arab Emirates officially formed in 1971, interest in restoring and preserving the country's artistic heritage has only grown. Abu Dhabi has taken the lead in this effort by opening galleries, sponsoring exhibits, and creating the Heritage Village outside Al-'Ayn. Dubai is also home to many galleries, and people can take classes in all types of art forms. To many people, however, it is Sharjah that is seen as the cultural capital of the United Arab Emirates. Often overlooked in favor of the two bigger UAE cities, some would say Sharjah takes the lead when it comes to arts and culture. Some even see it as the center of the arts for the entire Arab world, not just the UAE.

THE ART OF HENNA

One of the artistic techniques used for beauty purposes is dyeing hands—and often feet, ankles, and wrists—with henna. Henna is a natural dye that comes from the henna plant. It has been a favorite tool and beautification technique among women of the emirates for centuries. Today, henna-dyeing services are offered in beauty clinics around the country and have become popular with tourists.

The artistry is in the creation of beautifully intricate designs. Floral patterns are common, and so are abstract designs. These are usually applied to the hands as a beauty treatment. Henna dyeing is also associated with weddings. During the bride-to-be's prenuptial pampering, the patterns are applied to her wrists, ankles, and feet.

THE ART OF WEAVING

You may think of weaving as a technique used to make sweaters or thick blankets for cold climates, but even in the harsh desert environment, Bedu women display remarkable skill and artistry in weaving. They weave on simple looms, with the wool spooled around a wooden shuttle, which is then passed between the warp threads stretched between two wooden sticks. Traditionally,

HENNA ON THE HANDS

The red dye called henna is used in the traditional craft of hand-painting. Hand-painting is done for special occasions, especially marriage. It is increasingly popular with tourists and is now often used by people outside of the Arab world too.

The leaves of the henna shrub are ground into a fine powder using a mortar and pestle. This is then strained through a muslin cloth. The smooth powder is mixed with eucalyptus oil and lemon juice to make a paste.

The henna paste is applied to the hands or feet in intricate designs, usually floral in nature. Brides-to-be often have their hands, feet, wrists, and ankles decorated several days before the wedding ceremony.

Beauty clinics will do hand-painting for clients. The henna decorations can soften the skin and cool it against the harsh sunlight. The rich pigment can last on the skin for several weeks.

It is believed that henna has been used as an art form for at least 5,000 years.

the women used only natural dyes, such as sulfur, shells, and plants, including henna. However, in the mid- to late 1900s, artificial dyes began to be used. Today, artificial dyes have become common and in some cases are known to produce brighter colors.

With few animals, nomadic women use their resources carefully. Sheep's wool is generally used for furnishings and small rugs, while goat's wool is used mostly for tent cloth.

The patterns created are often strikingly beautiful, with geometric designs or stylized shapes of familiar objects commonly being used. Patterns are typically extended to the edge of the fabric rather than to a border. This is said to symbolize the endless horizon of the desert. The largest woven piece is the tent curtain. This is usually black and white, with the white being cotton purchased through trade. The curtain is narrow and runs from the back wall to the front, making a divider that provides privacy for women.

CULTURAL HERITAGE CENTERS

The Dubai International Arts Center in Jumeirah is one of the oldest private groups devoted to promoting traditional arts and crafts. Started in 1976, the center offers regular courses and demonstrations in both traditional and nontraditional art forms, such as interior decorating, photography, and painting. There are also courses in language and graphic design.

Emirate governments have established a number of heritage centers that, like the Dubai International Arts Center, provide courses and demonstrations. These centers are said to be the best sites for purchasing and learning about contemporary arts and crafts.

In an effort to preserve traditional crafts, both government and private agencies have established cultural centers, where crafts such as weaving are demonstrated, and lessons are offered.

British artist Sacha Jafri painted this work called *The Journey of Humanity* in Dubai in 2020 during the COVID-19 pandemic.

In spite of increasing interest, many of the craft items available for purchase in the UAE today are not indigenous but rather imported from other countries. The Emirati have been importing craft items since the earliest days of maritime trade, and this trade continues in the present. Tourists shopping in the souks bargain for such things as carpets from Iran, metalware from India, and jewelry from Oman. However, there are also some items made in the UAE. Many of the items sold in souks today are antiques. Examples of older items made in the UAE are found primarily in museums.

THE ART OF WEAPON-MAKING

Weapons were very important to Bedu men, not only as tools for fighting but as symbols of their family, clan, and tribe. They took great care of their weapons, using wet sand to keep them clean and free of rust, and even bestowing their favorites with pet names.

Swords and daggers were two of the most popular weapons to decorate elaborately. The short, curved dagger called a *khanjar* had intricate decorations and was carried in a silver scabbard. These are still worn by some men for special occasions. There are also several different sizes and shapes of daggers, with handles made of ivory or horn and decorations made of gold or silver.

By the 19th century, rifles and revolvers were important weapons. Revolver handles and rifle butts were elaborately carved or had stone inlays. Bows and arrows, including crossbows, were often decorated with seashell inlays.

JEWELRY

Most of the jewelry worn by Emirati women or sold in the souks is made in Oman and other countries. An exception is the practice among Bedu women of creating their own pieces out of coins, chains, beads, and other items purchased from village jewelers or from traveling merchants, including hajj pilgrims. Nearly all this jewelry is worn by women and children.

The people of what is now the UAE have been making pottery for more than 4,000 years. Pots and other vessels made out of the local red clay have traditionally been fired in a stone kiln lined with mud. Much of the pottery is made in Ra's al-Khaymah; some has also been imported from Oman and Iran.

Most of the pottery is quite plain and utilitarian, so it has not been a great attraction for tourists. Government efforts to revive the craft and create public exhibits have had modest success.

Although pottery made in the UAE is still often made from a practicality standpoint rather than an artistic standpoint, the works still sometimes include beautiful designs.

In the past, silver was the most highly prized form of jewelry because it was of great value. Women wore chains containing coins with a high silver content. Since the late 19th century, gold has become the favored metal, and it is also a major medium of international exchange. In Dubai and Abu Dhabi, entire souks are filled with shops dealing in gold jewelry.

The Gulf Arabs' fondness for practicality is displayed in their practice of giving a name to every handcrafted item that describes its precise function. In pottery, for example, pots called al-khers *are for storing food,* al-jarrah *are for carrying water from a well,* al-borma *are for cooking,* al-masaab *are for holding coffee, and* al-razem *are for holding or carrying coffee cups. There is also a special name—*al-haalool*—for vessels for giving water to wildlife.*

The same precision for naming is applied to items made from date palm leaves. Al-makhrafah, for instance, is a container in which dates are collected, while al-mezmah *is used to carry dates home, and* al-jefeer *are containers used to carry dates to a market.*

Traditionally, women own the jewelry they wear, but they can also act as the family's bank because many nomadic families often prefer to convert any money they have into jewelry rather than putting it in a bank.

MAKING DHOWS

Throughout history, the ancient craft of dhow-building has gone through several changes. Dhows were used for fishing, trade, and pearling for hundreds of years, each boat carefully made by hand. Some craftworkers on Dubai Creek and the outskirts of 'Ajmān continue to build them the traditional way. They work with wood and use very simple hand tools, such as planes, adzes, and chisels. Without using blueprints, the builders hand saw the main ribs out of single pieces of wood.

Dhows have been made in all sizes. The largest design, called a boom, had several large sails and was used for ocean trade to India and beyond. Some ancient booms have been converted into colorful, two-story restaurants. Smaller dhows, used in coastal trade, usually had a single, large, billowing sail, as well as a smaller one. Some had a raised deck, under which was a small cabin for the captain and crew. Others were completely open, with a canopy stretched over the length of the deck to protect the cargo, and sometimes the crew, from sun or rain.

In the early years of the oil boom, it seemed likely that dhows would become obsolete, replaced by more modern vessels. However, the ruling family of Dubai launched a revival of dhow-racing, and that triggered a new interest in the boats. Changes in technology also kept the craft alive. Fiberglass has become popular, replacing the wooden hulls, because it is lighter and more durable. Many modern dhows are also equipped with diesel engines as well as navigation aids such as radios and radar. Today, dhows are often used in tourism too. Visitors can take many different types of tours on dhows.

Today, dhows come in many different shapes and sizes. This traditional dhow is on display at the Dubai Museum.

MAKING MUSIC

Throughout history—and all over the world—songs and dances have provided welcome relief from hardship and monotony. This is especially true for the

This man and other musicians are shown here performing at a heritage festival in the art capital of the UAE, Sharjah.

desert-dwellers in what we now know as the UAE. Some of the music performed by people here expresses strong emotions, while other songs are made up of complex religious chants. Traditional music can still be heard on special occasions, such as at weddings or celebrations of National Day (December 2).

A wide variety of musical instruments were made from materials found in the desert or along the coast. Percussion instruments included the *jaser*, a drum made of goat skin on a wooden frame, which was hung around the neck. The *nisk* was made of coastal materials—a coconut sound box decorated with shells. The *sheklelah* was a tambourinelike instrument made of cloth and goat hooves and tied around the waist so that it clattered as the wearer moved. There were also wind instruments. One was a metal pipe wrapped with bands of copper. Another was a bamboo pipe with two rows of holes. There was

DANCE

Both music and dance strengthen the sense of belonging to a family, a clan, and a tribe. Some dances were used on the eve of war, even though warfare was usually in the form of a raid, rather than large battles.

A variety of folk dances are performed on special occasions, including weddings, and were traditionally performed on the return of the pearl divers. Some dances are related to Islam, including adaptations of narratives about the life of Muhammad.

Because of the region's long history of maritime trade, many dances have been introduced from other parts of the world too. For example, a dance called the lewa *originated in Africa. It uses large drums and has a very fast tempo.*

These men are performing a traditional dance in Abu Dhabi.

also a rosewood pipe wrapped with silver thread. Perhaps the most unusual instrument was a bagpipe made of goat skin, with a bamboo mouthpiece and goat hair tassels on the pipe. String instruments included a harplike instrument, made of wood and animal skin, and a simple wood violin.

Except for use on special occasions, these instruments have been replaced by electronic guitars and synthesizers. Night clubs and hotels organize special evenings of Arabic music. These events, which often run all night, also include more modern Middle Eastern songs. Usually, the audience becomes involved, dancing with their hands in the air. Belly dancing, which originated in Egypt, is also popular.

A number of contemporary UAE singers have become popular throughout the Persian Gulf. Ahlam is considered the first Arab female pop star. Other popular singers are Samar, Reem, and Abdallah Belkhair.

THE ART OF WORDS

Poetry is part of the emirates' long oral tradition, dating back more than a thousand years, and is often associated with music. Verses were recited in a singsong voice or sung, often accompanied by musical instruments. As with music and dance, poetry is often centered around religion.

Within the last several decades, a number of writers in the UAE have become the pioneers of a new literary age. Mohammed al-Murr, for example, has emerged as one of the UAE's leading fiction writers. His book *The Wink of the Mona Lisa* is a collection of 24 short stories. In addition, a number of leading figures have written books about the country's economic miracle, including Mohammed al-Fahim's *From Rags to Riches, A Story of Abu Dhabi*.

THE MANY ART FORMS

Whether one prefers dancing, singing, carving, drawing, painting, or one of the many other art forms that exist, there is likely a place for them to do it in the UAE. From the bigger cultural heritage centers to smaller, local organizations, classes and studios can be found around the country, especially in the major

cities of Dubai, Abu Dhabi, and Sharjah. Even for those who do not consider themselves artists, it's not hard to appreciate the beautiful art all around the UAE. Just head to one of the many souks around the country and you will find dozens of vendors and a vast assortment of beautiful artwork.

This man in Abu Dhabi is creating intricate designs on his works of art.

INTERNET LINKS

www.artdubai.com
The official website of the Dubai International Art Center has many resources. You can even read about the center's current exhibitions.

www.pbs.org/independentlens/newamericans/culturalriches/art_henna.html
Read about the cultural practice and art of henna here.

LEISURE

This man is sandboarding on a dune known as Big Red. It is near Dubai.

ONCE AGAIN, OIL WEALTH IS A KEY driving force behind another aspect of daily life in the United Arab Emirates: leisure. Before the discovery of oil here, few people had either the time or money to enjoy leisure activities. Today, that has largely changed. Tourists also benefit from the many popular leisure activities available in the emirates. Visitors often come for family vacations, and a growing number of people from around the world are purchasing vacation homes in the UAE. While in the country, many enjoy leisure activities unique to the region. Businesspeople in the country from other nations also often enjoy these activities, with many balancing work with pleasure.

Some would say that the only drawback to the sun-filled climate in the UAE is that it makes the summer heat so oppressive that people tend to avoid it as much as possible. However, with modern technology, there are many alternatives, including air-conditioned malls, theaters, and restaurants, as well as shaded parks, fountains, and pools.

"I don't like to see someone who does not have a hobby, sport or passion in life. Idleness is not only an attitude towards work; it starts with the mind." —Sheikh Muhammad ibn Rāshid al-Maktūm

FAMILY TIME

A good deal of people's leisure time involves traditional activities mixed with the new and modern. Social visits remain a favorite pastime, for example. It's common for these visits to involve coffee or tea and light refreshments. While these visits usually take place in someone's home, the availability of air-conditioned cafés and coffee shops offers an inviting alternative way to get together.

Families also take advantage of the variety of parks, green spaces, and pools scattered throughout the cities. Many parks have family-oriented features, such as barbecue pits, play areas for children, and swimming pools with lifeguards. Beaches are also a favorite gathering spot for local families and tourists alike. The beautiful sand beaches extend for miles, and many are equipped with beach umbrellas or palm trees for shade. Jumeirah Beach is reserved for women and children on certain days, and Al-Dana Beach is solely for women and children. Because of traditional Islamic beliefs and clothing requirements, Muslim women often do not go swimming in front of men. These beach days for women and children only provide a time and a place for them to be able to swim comfortably.

SHOP TIL YOU DROP

The three major cities of the UAE are rapidly making the UAE one of the world's greatest shopping centers. Dubai even has an annual shopping festival.

An almost endless array of goods is available, from the latest electronic marvels to antique copperware and intricate rugs. While locally made crafts are hard to find, there is an abundance from throughout southern Asia. There are also designer shops, featuring labels from Paris, London, and New York. The malls and shops are open early and close late. Most also close for three hours during the hottest part of the day.

A more traditional kind of shopping takes place in the souks, where narrow alleys lead to merchant shops and stalls. Many people prefer shopping in the souks, partly because they are reminders of a proud history, and some like

In their bid to bring tourist dollars to the UAE while also providing fun for nationals, the emirates have created several colossal amusement parks. Dubai has led the way with the Wonder Land Theme and Water Park, featuring water slides and a number of large rides with varying levels of thrill. In 2016, Dubai opened a record-setting amusement park. When IMG Worlds of Adventure opened, it was dubbed "the world's largest indoor theme park." It's around 1.5 million square feet (139,350 sq m) and is about as big as 28 football fields!

Other popular amusement parks in the UAE include Adventureland in Sharjah, Dreamland Aqua Park in Umm al-Qaywayn, and Ferrari World in Abu Dhabi.

Wild Wadi Waterpark in Dubai, near Jumeirah, is a perfect place for families to cool off outside in the hot summer sun.

the fun of haggling over prices. In addition, shoppers may happen upon unique items, and there are tailor shops that can recreate any article of expensive designer clothing at a fraction of the cost.

GET GOLFING

In February 2006, hundreds of spectators lined the course as golf great Tiger Woods stormed from behind to tie for the lead and then win the tournament in a one-hole playoff. The tournament was the Dubai Desert Classic, which

Woods would win again in 2008. Today, the tournament continues to draw some of the world's' best golfers to the UAE.

Golf is just one of many sports that have gained popularity in recent years in the UAE. The people of the emirates, as well as foreign visitors, are taking advantage of the wide array of sports facilities becoming available. Some of the sports are traditional. Others, such as golf, are newer to the UAE. Big events, such as the Dubai Desert Classic, are bringing spectators as well as participants to the country.

HEAD TO THE HORSES

Sheikh Muhammad, the president of Dubai, is typical of the newer generation of sports enthusiasts, loving both the traditional and the new. He has the reputation of being a good ruler with ambitious plans for his emirate, and he is a man of many talents. He has written poetry, but he has also gained an international reputation in a vastly different field—the sport of endurance horse-racing! Sheikh Muhammad has even taken part in 70-mile (112 km) horse-racing marathons across the desert. The entire al-Maktoum family, rulers of Dubai, has taken a leading role in promoting horse racing. The family members want the UAE to be a center for Thoroughbred training and racing. They point out that every Thoroughbred horse racing today can trace its lineage to Arabian stallions, which were exported to Britain three centuries ago.

Today, the Dubai World Cup, held each year since 1996, is one of the biggest horse races in the world. Some of the best riders in the world come to Dubai to take part in the race every year. The race was established by Sheikh Muhammad, and the al-Maktoum family has put billions of dollars into establishing the Al Quoz Stables and in improving training facilities. They have built a great racing complex with a stadium, a grass track and a sand track, and a golf course in the enormous infield. They have more than 1,000 Thoroughbreds training in Europe and North America, as well as in Dubai.

The UAE's interest in horseback riding is not limited to the high-profile races. There are several smaller racetracks scattered throughout the country. In addition, there are many facilities for horseback riding, including places offering lessons for beginners.

ANOTHER TYPE OF RACING

Horse races might seem pretty familiar to you, but here's a type of racing you may have never heard of: camel racing. Camel racing is actually a sport with a long history that has experienced a new flurry of interest in recent years in the UAE. The sport is popular throughout the country, with races run on both circular and straight tracks. The races, commonly held on Fridays and public holidays, are noisy affairs because supporters drive behind the camels in four-wheel-drive vehicles to urge them on.

Training is often put in the hands of Bedu, who specialize in breeding and training racing camels. They prepare the camels for the racing season, which runs from September to late April, and each trainer feeds his animals a special concoction, usually including alfalfa, barley, ghee (clarified butter), honey, and dates.

The jockeys are commonly children because of their light weight. Children as young as six or seven are sometimes riders. The camels reach speeds of 37 miles (60 km) per hour! The lure of winning prize money draws many children to try out for jobs as jockeys.

Riders and their camels line up for the start of a camel race in the UAE.

THE SPORT OF FALCONRY

Falconry has been a favorite sport of desert sheikhs for many centuries. Falcons have been trained to hunt doves, sandgrouse, and the houbara bustard bird. The sport is even more popular today among the wealthy. Falcon clubs for exercising and training the beautiful, intelligent birds are found on the outskirts of most cities and towns.

The hunting season lasts from October to January, which is also the time of autumn bird migrations. Falcons are purchased from Iran, Pakistan, and other countries and range in price from hundreds to tens of thousands of dollars. The price depends on several factors, including the length of the tail feathers, an indicator of flying ability. Females, being one-third larger than males, are generally preferred.

The standard equipment for falconry includes the leather glove, or *mangalah*, worn by the falconer for protection against the bird's sharp talons. When resting, the falcon perches on a *wakir*, a highly decorated pole, and the head is covered with a leather hood.

Those who practice falconry are known as falconers. In the UAE, many often practice in groups in the desert.

Because the terrain of al-Fujayrah, the easternmost emirate, is not conducive for camel racing, bullfighting has long been a popular substitute as a spectator sport. This is not bullfighting in the style of Spain or Mexico, in which a lone matador confronts a bull. Instead, this is a contest of one 2,000-pound (907 kilogram) Brahma bull fighting another.

The bulls, long used for work in the emirates' palm groves, are bred for strength and raised on a diet of grain, honey, and milk. The goal of the fight is for one bull to force the other to the ground. A bull can also win by forcing its opponent to flee. The age of the sport is unknown. The bulls may have been introduced by the Portuguese in the 16th century, but the sport itself may date back to before 1000 CE in Persia.

Hunting expeditions have always been elaborate affairs organized by sheikhs and consist of 20 or more people. Most trips are now made in four-wheel-drive vehicles. Once bird tracks are identified, a camp is set up, and the hunters go to work. The falcons are incredibly swift. One of the largest species, the saker, uses its keen intelligence to predict the movements of its prey and uses the landscape to disguise its own movements.

SPECTATOR SPORTS AND CASUAL RECREATION

Like in the rest of the world, many popular sports in the UAE are geared toward spectators as well as participants. Some sports have been promoted in Dubai to draw sports enthusiasts from around the world. In addition to the golf tournament, the emirate hosts the Dubai Tennis Championships, bringing many of the world's top tennis players to the UAE. For recreational participants, tennis courts are available throughout the emirates.

A number of smaller events are useful for introducing the people of the UAE to new sports. Car races, bowling championships, football (called soccer in the United States), and rugby are all available. Sharjah has even been host to the World Masters cricket tournament. Thanks to certain cooling technologies, ice-skating rinks are also becoming popular in this hot country, and ice hockey is emerging as a new spectator sport.

The clear waters of the Persian Gulf and its sunshine invite an amazing variety of water sports. Water sports include sailing (shown below), surfing and windsurfing, snorkeling, and water-skiing. There has also been a revival of dhow racing. The rulers of the UAE organize several races, including the annual President's Cup Regatta, which is also known as the Dubai-Muscat Offshore Sailing Race. There are also a variety of dhow excursions for fishing, scuba diving, or watching dolphins.

Some people prefer to casually take part in sports and activities. Rather than training hard for competitions, they do it for fun. If you're looking for a new activity to try, the UAE is the place to find it! In the deserts, sandboarding has been popular and is a common activity for tourists. It's similar to snowboarding but participants ride down a sand dune instead of a hill of snow.

Speaking of snowboarding, you may have thought snow sports couldn't be done in a desert. The people behind Ski Dubai have found a way around that, however. It takes serious air-conditioning to keep all the snow frozen, but it's worth it for all the skiers and snowboarders who shred down the many indoor slopes.

At Ski Dubai, there are slopes and activities for skiers and snowboarders of all different levels. There's even an indoor ski lift.

INTERNET LINKS

www.dubairacingclub.com/visit/racing-season/dubai-world-cup
Learn more about the Dubai World Cup and other horse races in the area here.

www.imgworlds.com/language/en/#
Check out all the rides and entertainment available at the IMG Worlds of Adventure Theme Park.

www.omegadubaidesertclassic.com/
This is the official website for the Dubai Desert Classic Golf Tournament.

FESTIVALS

This mosque is beautifully lit as part of a lights festival in Sharjah.

12

THE UNITED ARAB EMIRATES IS A country full of culture, and with culture often comes festivals. Since the UAE is a fairly new country, there are few secular holidays commemorating historical events. However, one particularly notable exception is National Day, celebrated on December 2, marking the day the UAE formally came together as one nation. The day stands for unity and togetherness and is commonly marked with fireworks, fairs, and sporting events such as horse races.

In addition, several of the emirates have special days to honor their ruling sheikh. For many years, for example, Abu Dhabi marked August 6 as a holiday, celebrating the accession of Sheikh Zāyid. New Year's Day—January 1—is also a secular holiday. The influx of people from other parts of the world has also brought a diverse array of popular festivals from other cultures and countries to the UAE.

On National Day, the colors of the UAE flag can be found all around the country, from people's clothing to decorations on homes, streets, and cars.

FAMILY TIES

As in other cultures, family festivals follow major events in the life cycle—birthdays, marriage, the birth of children, and death. There are numerous traditions associated with these events, many of them stemming from Bedu desert life, others from Islamic practices.

Marriage announcements are issued verbally by women, while men announce the event in the mosque. The Bedu tradition of hospitality is highlighted in the wedding feast. Separate dining tents are established for men and women, and a special kitchen is set up to prepare mountains of food. Guests are encouraged to take away food parcels to give to any friends or relatives who could not attend.

The birth of a child is also an occasion for great celebration. Births take place in the modern, well-equipped hospitals located throughout the UAE. The hospital births have greatly reduced the previously high infant mortality rate, and families have adjusted their celebrations to fit the new hospital environment. Visitors now bring their presents and special foods to the hospital, and the halls are filled with colorful bouquets. All the new mothers and families on the same ward congratulate each other, even though they have probably never met before.

For Muslims, death is usually not an occasion for extended mourning. If possible, the deceased is buried on the day of death, with the body placed on its side, facing Mecca. Forty days after death, close family members hold a feast to celebrate the deceased's ascent into heaven.

IMPORTANT ISLAMIC FESTIVALS

Islam has a number of holidays throughout the year. These generally follow the Islamic calendar, which is based on the phases of the moon, so their dates change by a few days each year.

The most important period in Islam is the month of Ramadan, the ninth month in the lunar calendar. Faithful Muslims observe a strict fast every day of the month during daylight hours. After sunset, there are dinners, prayers, and business meetings that can extend far into the night. These evenings are

Great feasts are part of most festivals in the UAE. Frequently, the meals center around what is called ouzi, *meaning "live cooking." This usually consists of fresh lamb, cooked outdoors on a spit or in an oven until the meat is very tender. The lamb can be stuffed with a mixture of rice, spices, raisins, and nuts.*

A tradition for any special occasion is the fou-alla, *consisting of a platter of delicate sweets, served with coffee or tea. The meal ends with women burning a variety of incense.*

also important times for majlis, when citizens can express their views to their ruler or petition him for some special act or favor.

The month of Ramadan is followed by a great festival called Eid al-Fitr, the Feast of the Fast Breaking, held during the first four days of the month of Shawwal. People enjoy festive meals, exchange gifts, take part in family or community prayers, and hold important business meetings. This is another time for majlis, when tribal leaders and business executives visit the people who depend on them to resolve any problems.

Other Islamic holidays include days to honor the ascension of the Prophet, the Prophet's birthday, and the Islamic New Year. Another festival, Eid al-Adha, takes place during the month of the hajj—the pilgrimage to Mecca.

OTHER RELIGIOUS FESTIVALS

The large Hindu population, made up of immigrants from India, celebrates a variety of occasions. These vary according to what part of India the people came from. Many of the festivals include religious ceremonies mixed with processions, demonstrations of magic, feasting, and a number of fun-filled activities. During the spring Holi festival, for example, which is designed to revive the powers of nature, participants throw colored powder and water at each other.

In Hindu festivals celebrating the New Year, objects representing the sickness and "impurities" of the past year are thrown into a bonfire. People also celebrate the coming of the New Year by forgiving debts owed to them,

Holi is an ancient Hindu festival also known as the "festival of spring" or the "festival of colors." People are shown here celebrating Holi in Dubai.

paying their own debts, and trying to resolve any lingering conflicts or problems. In one variation of New Year celebrations, ceremonial lights honor Laksmi, the goddess of wealth and good fortune. During the days of this October festival, fireworks are set off to chase away evil spirits, and people engage in several kinds of gambling, which is designed to bring good luck.

While Christians are a minority in the UAE, there is still a large enough number of them that it is not uncommon to see Christian holidays and festivals happening throughout the country. While it is not a national holiday and most people do not celebrate it in a religious way, Christmas decorations have actually become surprisingly popular in the UAE. Due to the country's large foreign population, with many coming from countries where Christmas is celebrated even by those who are not strictly religious, malls, hotels, and other public spaces often decorate for Christmas.

OTHER KINDS OF FESTIVALS

Not all big festivals are based around religion. There are festivals for sports, arts, dance, and music. Other big festivals celebrate lasting UAE traditions, in which religion does play a role, but the festivals themselves are not necessarily based in religion. The Al Dhafra Festival, for example, is held annually in Abu Dhabi and is a showcase of the Bedu lifestyle. Each year, more than 25,000 camels come to the area near the edge of the Empty Quarter. Popular events include camel racing, date packing, falconry, and even a camel beauty contest!

These men share a meal of camel and rice at a camel festival.

INTERNET LINKS

abudhabiculture.ae/en/experience/heritage-festivals/al-dhafra-festival
See pictures and learn more about the Al Dhafra festival here.

www.bbc.com/news/av/business-16224148
Watch a video and see how various places in the UAE decorate for Christmas.

www.dkfindout.com/us/more-find-out/festivals-and-holidays/ramadan/
Go to this interactive page to learn more about Ramadan.

www.nationalgeographic.org/media/holi-festival/
Learn more about the Hindu festival of Holi here.

FOOD

With advanced water systems, many types of produce are now grown in the UAE. Some fruits and vegetables are imported from other countries too.

13

WHILE EMIRATIS HAVE MANY wonderful food-related traditions of their own, the United Arab Emirates has become a place known for its international cuisine. The UAE's long history of international trade is part of the reason why locals and visitors alike can now enjoy a wonderful mixing of foods and recipes from all over the world. The oil boom brought people from places such as India, Pakistan, and the Philippines. Each group brought with them some of their own unique and delicious recipes and foods. When the tourism industry began to boom, restaurants serving all sorts of Western cuisines, such as French, Italian, and even fast foods from the United States, began to open up all over the large cities too.

Many food-related traditions and cuisines from the UAE came from the Bedu lifestyle. For example, the Bedu ate from a communal plate, using the right hand. This form of communal eating, which is also sanctioned by the teachings of the Prophet Muhammad, is still common throughout the Arab world and the UAE today.

TRADITIONAL UAE FOOD AND MEALS

Before the changes introduced by the oil boom, Emirati families ate the foods available to them, including several imported items, such as basmati rice from Pakistan. Fish, lamb, goat, and dates were standard. Meat was cooked on a grill or barbecue and seasoned with local spices, including cardamom, cumin, and coriander. Other imported flavorings were chili, ginger, cinnamon, nutmeg, and saffron.

One of the unique flavors of traditional cooking was imparted by dried limes. These imported limes, found in Oman and Asian countries such as Thailand, are dried on the tree and are still used in many recipes.

These men are preparing bread to be eaten at the Iftar meal during Ramadan.

BEDU DIET

Since the Bedu were travelers, they had to look for food that they could find wherever they were. For this reason, their diet often relied on the animals that walked with them. Traditionally, the diet of the nomadic Bedu relied heavily on the camel. Bedu drank camel milk either hot or cold. Sometimes it was even boiled with bread or cooked with rice to make more of a meal. They ate meat occasionally, often by trading goods of their own for sheep or goat meat. Near the coast, they could purchase fresh or dried fish, such as sun-dried sardines. In the Bedu culture, nothing is to be wasted. Non-meat parts of animals could be used for clothing or building materials. For meals, an entire sheep would be served on a bed of rice. The men would eat first, then the women. The children were able to have what was left.

Today, oil wealth has made possible the importation of a wide range of fresh fruits and vegetables. The governments of the emirates have also devoted sizable resources to increasing domestic food production, including fruits, eggs, and dairy products.

A typical breakfast, or *fatoor*, is likely to consist of fresh fruit or juice, eggs, pita (unleavened bread), jam or honey, and coffee or tea. Lunch (*ghu daa*) is the main meal of the day. Fish, chicken, or another kind of meat is usually served with rice and fresh herbs, followed by dates and other fruits. Dinner, or *aa sha*, is often a lighter meal of pita bread and cheese or meat, with eggs or soup, followed by fruit and tea or coffee.

THE COFFEE CEREMONY

The traditional UAE coffee, called kahwa, is offered to guests as a symbol of hospitality and is also an important component of midday meals. The traditional method of preparing coffee involves roasting the beans in a frying pan, then grinding them with a mortar and pestle, and boiling them. Today, it is quite acceptable to buy coffee that has already been roasted and ground. The boiled coffee is poured over a mixture of cardamom, cloves, and saffron, creating a light, fairly sweet, and aromatic coffee.

In the tourist-oriented cities of the UAE, almost every form of international cuisine is available. The four- and five-star hotels offer European and North American foods, including French, Italian, German, Hungarian, and American Creole, as well as Mexican.

Abu Dhabi, Dubai, and Sharjah also have more modestly priced restaurants featuring the cuisines of India, Pakistan, Thailand, and the Philippines. In addition, Arabic restaurants offer such specialties as shawarma—*chicken, beef, or lamb roasted on a spit—and falafel—patties made of ground chickpeas and served with pita pockets.*

Coffee is poured from a pot called a *dallah* and is served in tiny cups without handles. After having two to three cups, it is acceptable to refuse another refill, normally by shaking the cup from side to side.

Traditional UAE coffee shops seem to be disappearing, often replaced by modern European and American coffeehouses. A few of the old-style shops are still found in the souks, and the coffee ceremony is still practiced in people's homes.

RESTAURANT DINING

Many of the UAE's restaurants, including those in luxurious hotels, serve buffets for both lunch and dinner. This style is common throughout the Middle East, especially in Lebanese restaurants, which are very popular in the emirates.

Lebanese restaurants usually serve a dazzling array of 25 to 30 small dishes with dips, called *meze*. These are followed by a main course, but many diners limit themselves to meze.

Several meze dishes are extremely popular. Tabbouleh, for example, is an herb salad made with bulgur wheat, mixed with chopped parsley, onions, tomato, and mint. Hummus is also popular. This is a paste made of mashed chickpeas mixed with tahini (sesame and garlic paste), olive oil, and lemon juice. In the UAE, hummus is sometimes topped with minced lamb. Another delicious dish is *moutabel*, which is made from eggplant.

All of these dips or spreads are eaten with pita bread or a variation called *mafrooda*, an almost-white bread without a pocket that is held in the right hand and used as a scoop to pick up the meze. A variety of fresh vegetables is also sometimes used for picking up the dips.

The main course often consists of chicken or lamb kebabs. Many kinds of fish are also cut into chunks and served as kebabs. Shrimp, or prawns, and other forms of seafood are also common.

EATING ON THE GO

There are many different fast foods available in the UAE. The Arabic shawarma can be topped with yogurt or tahini and served in a pita pocket, to be eaten

Tourists and locals alike enjoy eating along Dubai's waterfront.

like a sandwich. Falafel, too, is often sold by street vendors and served in a paper bag.

European and American fast foods are also popular. Hamburgers, pizza, fish and chips, and other foods typical of American and British restaurant chains are available in the shopping malls of the three major cities. The towns of the smaller emirates, such as Ra's al-Khaymah, al-Fujayrah, and Umm al-Qaywayan, have not embraced fast foods nearly as much as those that are home to more visitors.

Fast-food restaurants have become popular around the world so that people can eat on the go whenever they want. When leading a busy lifestyle, this helps with convenience. As the major cities of the United Arab Emirates have become more business-oriented and popular with tourists, the fast-food industry has gained traction here. Still, it is important for people to slow down sometimes and enjoy their mealtimes. One way families come together is to sit down and enjoy traditional meals. While international cuisine and fast-food restaurants have popped up, enjoying a traditional family meal is still very much commonplace for people living in the United Arab Emirates. Whether the meal is in celebration of a special occasion or just because, gathering together to dine is an important part of Emirati culture, as it is for many cultures around the world.

During Ramadan, coming together to break the fast during Iftar is an important tradition. This photo shows some of the foods you may see on an Iftar table.

INTERNET LINKS

www.bbc.co.uk/bitesize/articles/z4cmkmn
Learn about the different foods people around the world eat during Eid al-Fitr.

www.dayoutdubai.ae/blog/safari/traditional-food-of-uae/
Read about more traditional Emirati foods on this website.

theculturetrip.com/middle-east/united-arab-emirates/articles/a-beginners-guide-to-emirati-cuisine/
This article offers a crash course on popular cuisine in the UAE.

CHEBAB BREAD

Also known as an Emirati pancake, Chebab bread is often served for breakfast or dinner in the UAE. This recipe serves four.

3 cups flour
¼ cup sugar
½ teaspoon salt
1 teaspoon yeast
½ teaspoon cardamom powder
A few dashes of saffron
1 cup (237 milliliters) milk
2 eggs

Mix the flour, sugar, salt, yeast, cardamom powder, and saffron together in a bowl. Next, pour the milk into the mixture. In a separate bowl, whisk the eggs. Add the whisked eggs to the mixture, and mix everything together. The batter should be similar to the consistency of pancake batter. If needed, you can add small amounts of water, little by little, until the consistency seems right. Let the batter sit for an hour.

For the next step, you can either use a nonstick pan or grease your pan. Have an adult help you heat the pan on the stove. Scoop a spoonful of the batter onto the pan and cook on medium heat. Flip, and cook the other side. When both sides are a golden brown color, remove from the pan. You can then add butter, honey, or other toppings, and enjoy!

AL HAREES

This is a popular Arabic dish made with wheat and chicken. It's commonly served at special occasions, such as at weddings or during Ramadan. You need to start this recipe a day before you plan to eat it, by soaking the wheat overnight.

2 cups of whole wheat harees grains
2 pounds (0.9 kg) of chicken, deboned
2 cinnamon sticks
1 teaspoon black pepper powder
Salt to taste
Melted butter or olive oil

In a large pot, add the soaked wheat, chicken, cinnamon, black pepper, salt, and enough water so it comes to about 1 to 2 inches (2.5 to 5 centimeters) above the mixture. Bring the pot's contents to a boil. Continue to cook until the harees becomes a watery consistency, stirring every few minutes and making sure to get the bottom of the pot to prevent the contents from getting burnt.

Once cooked, you will need a hand blender. Blend the meal enough so that it is mixed but still a little bit grainy. Add butter or olive oil on top, and serve!

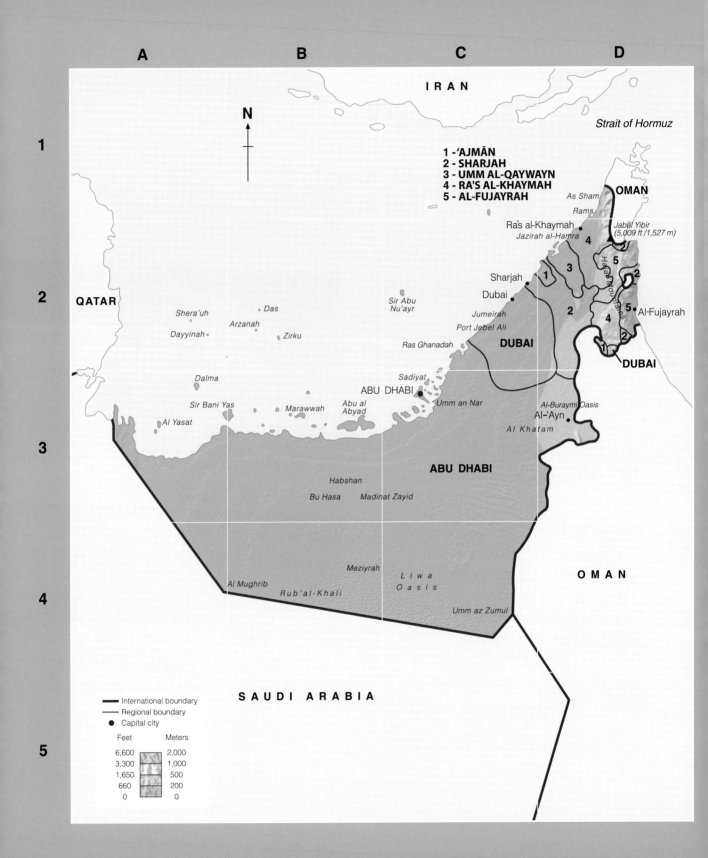

Abu al Abyad, B3

Abu Dhabi, A3—A4, B3—B4, C2—C4, D3

'Ajmān, D2

Al-'Ayn, D3

Al-Buraymi Oasis, D3

Al-Fujayrah, D2

Al Khatam, C3, D3

Al Mughrib, B4

Al Yasat, A3

As Sham, D1

Arzanah, B2

Bu Hasa, B3

Dalma, A3

Das, B2

Dayyinah, A2

Dubai, C2—C3, D2, D3

Habshan, B3

Hajar Mountains, D2

Iran, B1, C1, D1

Jabal Yibir, D2

Jazirah al-Hamra, D2

Jumeirah, C2

Liwa Oasis, B4, C4

Madinat Zayid, B3

Marawwah, B3

Meziyrah, B4

Oman, D1—D5, C4

Persian Gulf, A1—A3, B1—B3, C1—C3, D1

Port Jebel Ali, C2

Qatar, A1, A2

Rams, D1

Ra's al-Khaymah, D1—D2

Ras Ghanadah, C2

Rub 'al-Khali, B4

Sadiyat, C3

Saudi Arabia, A3—A5, B4—B5, C4—C5, D4—D5

Sharjah, C2, D2—D3

Shera'uh, A2

Sir Abu Nu'ayr, C2

Sir Bani Yas, A3, B3

Strait of Hormuz, D1

Umm al-Qaywayn, D2

Umm an Nar, C3

Umm az Zumul, C4

Zirku, B2

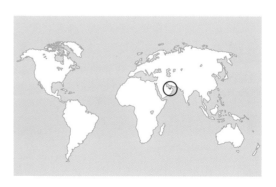

ECONOMIC
UNITED ARAB EMIRATES

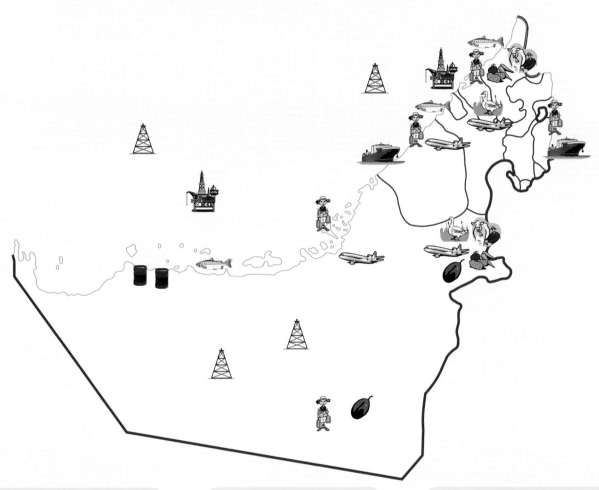

Natural Resources

 Oil Field

 Oil Refinery

 Natural gas

 Fish

Services

 Airport

 Seaport

 Tourism

Agriculture

 Dates

 Other fruits, vegetables

 Poultry

 Dairy products

ABOUT THE ECONOMY

All figures are 2021 estimates unless otherwise noted.

GROSS DOMESTIC PRODUCT
$421.077 billion (2019)

PER CAPITA GDP
$67,119 (2019)

GDP GROWTH RATE
0.8 percent (2017)

GDP BY SECTOR
agriculture 0.8 percent, industry 49.8 percent, services 49.2 percent (2017)

AGRICULTURAL PRODUCTS
dates, other fruits, vegetables, poultry, eggs, dairy products, fish

INDUSTRIAL PRODUCTS
oil refining, aluminum, textiles, petrochemicals, handicrafts, construction materials

INFLATION RATE
-1.9 percent (2019)

CURRENCY
Dirham (AED)
USD $1 = 3.67 Dirham

WORKFORCE
5.344 million (2017)

WORKFORCE BY SECTOR
agriculture 7 percent, industry 15 percent, services 78 percent

UNEMPLOYMENT RATE
1.6 percent (2016)

MAIN EXPORTS
crude oil, natural gas, dates, dried fish

MAIN IMPORTS
machinery, transportation equipment, chemicals, food

MAIN TRADE PARTNERS
Japan, India, China, Iran, Oman, Switzerland, South Korea, United States

CULTURAL UNITED ARAB EMIRATES

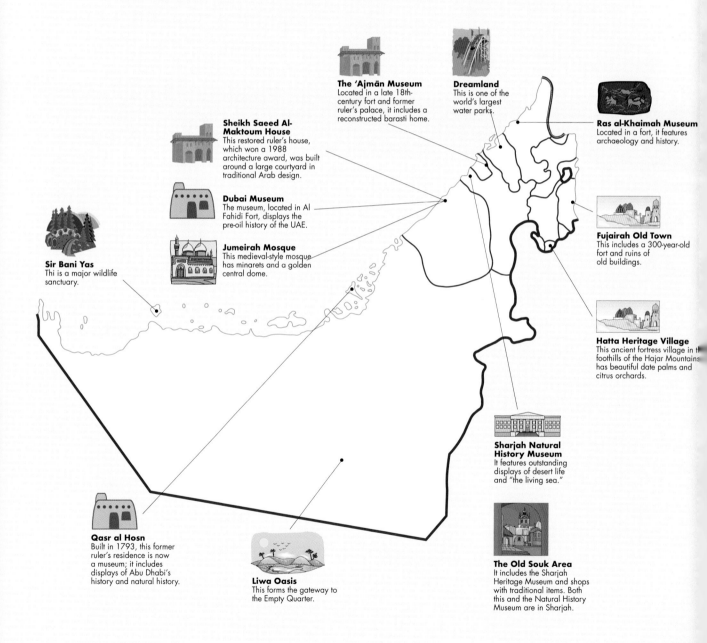

The 'Ajmān Museum
Located in a late 18th-century fort and former ruler's palace, it includes a reconstructed barasti home.

Dreamland
This is one of the world's largest water parks.

Ras al-Khaimah Museum
Located in a fort, it features archaeology and history.

Sheikh Saeed Al-Maktoum House
This restored ruler's house, which won a 1988 architecture award, was built around a large courtyard in traditional Arab design.

Dubai Museum
The museum, located in Al Fahidi Fort, displays the pre-oil history of the UAE.

Jumeirah Mosque
This medieval-style mosque has minarets and a golden central dome.

Fujairah Old Town
This includes a 300-year-old fort and ruins of old buildings.

Sir Bani Yas
Thi is a major wildlife sanctuary.

Hatta Heritage Village
This ancient fortress village in th foothills of the Hajar Mountains has beautiful date palms and citrus orchards.

Sharjah Natural History Museum
It features outstanding displays of desert life and "the living sea."

Qasr al Hosn
Built in 1793, this former ruler's residence is now a museum; it includes displays of Abu Dhabi's history and natural history.

Liwa Oasis
This forms the gateway to the Empty Quarter.

The Old Souk Area
It includes the Sharjah Heritage Museum and shops with traditional items. Both this and the Natural History Museum are in Sharjah.

All figures are 2021 estimates unless otherwise noted.

OFFICIAL NAME
United Arab Emirates

POPULATION
9,856,612

CAPITAL
Abu Dhabi

ETHNIC GROUPS
Emirati 11.6 percent, South Asians 59.4 percent, Egyptian 10.2 percent, Filipino 6 percent, other 12.8 percent

LIFE EXPECTANCY
81 years for women, 78 years for men

RELIGIONS
Muslim 76 percent, Christian 9 percent, other (primarily Hindu and Buddhist) 15 percent

LANGUAGES
Arabic (official), English, Persian, Hindi, Urdu

LITERACY RATE
93.8 percent

NATIONAL HOLIDAY
National Day (December 2)

LEADERS IN POLITICS
President: Sheikh Khalīfah ibn Zāyid Al Nahyān
Vice president and prime minister: Sheikh Muhammad ibn Rāshid al-Maktūm

TIMELINE

IN UNITED ARAB EMIRATES	IN THE WORLD
5000–3000 BCE There is evidence of human settlements on the coast and inland.	
3000 BCE The region supplies copper to civilizations in Mesopotamia.	**3000–1520 BCE** Stonehenge is built.
2500–2000 BCE Maritime trade develops.	**323 BCE** Alexander the Great's empire stretches from Greece to India.
630–640 CE Islam comes to the region.	
700–900 Seafaring trade to India and China develops.	**1000 CE** The Chinese perfect gunpowder and begin to use it in warfare.
	1100 The rise of the Inca civilization occurs in Peru.
	1206–1368 Genghis Khan unifies the Mongols and starts their conquest of the world.
1500–1600 Portugal controls Persian Gulf trade.	**1558–1603** The reign of Elizabeth I of England takes place.
1700–1800 Qawasim tribe of Ra's al-Khaymah controls many Gulf ports.	
1761 Abu Dhabi is first settled.	**1776** U.S. Declaration of Independence is signed.
	1789–1799 The French Revolution occurs.
1820 British forces attack Qawasim ports. British sign the General Treaty of Peace with the emirates.	
1833 Bani Yas tribe establishes Dubai, ruled by the al-Maktoum family.	
1853 The Perpetual Peace is signed, with the British providing protection to all the Trucial States.	**1861** The American Civil War begins.
	1914 World War I begins.

IN UNITED ARAB EMIRATES	IN THE WORLD
1936–1952 Rulers of the Trucial States sign oil agreements with Western oil companies.	**1939** World War II begins.
	1949 The North Atlantic Treaty Organization (NATO) is formed.
1958 Oil is discovered in Abu Dhabi.	
1971 Britain withdraws from the Persian Gulf. United Arab Emirates is formed on December 2.	
1972 Ra's al-Khaymah joins the UAE in February.	
1973 OPEC (Organization of Petroleum Exporting Countries) quadruples crude oil prices.	**1974** Richard Nixon becomes the first U.S. president to resign, after the Watergate scandal.
1980 Iran-Iraq War begins.	
1996 The first Dubai World Cup is held.	**1991** The breakup of the Soviet Union happens.
2004 Sheikh Zāyid ibn Sulṭān Al Nahyān dies on November 2.	**2001** Terrorists crash planes in New York, Washington, D.C., and Pennsylvania.
2010 The tallest building in the world, the Burj Khalifa, is completed in Dubai	**2008** Barack Obama is elected as the first Black president of the United States.
2015 Over a quarter of the members of the FNC are women.	**2016** The Olympics are held in South America for the first time, in Rio de Janeiro, Brazil.
2018 Marking 100 years since Sheikh Zāyid's birth, the year is claimed the "Year of Zāyid."	
2019 By the order of Sheikh Khalīfah, 50 percent of FNC members are women.	**2020** Countries all over the world shut down due to COVID-19.

GLOSSARY

aba
The traditional dress of Arab women.

barasti
The traditional house of the region's people, with a common room in front and a private room in the rear.

blasphemy
An act of disrespect shown toward a god or something holy.

burka
A covering of the nose and mouth, worn by some Muslim women.

dhow
The traditional boat of the Persian Gulf and much of Africa.

dialect
A form of a language spoken in a particular area that uses some of its own words, grammar, and pronunciations.

dishdash
The traditional long garment or robe worn by Emirati men.

dugong
Also known as a sea cow—a large, slow-moving sea mammal, related to the manatee of North America.

emir
A sheikh or ruler; source of the word "emirate."

Emirati
The nationals of the United Arab Emirates.

falaj
An ancient system of irrigation, using stone-lined channels.

hajj
The Muslim pilgrimage to Mecca.

majlis
The traditional communication between a sheikh and his subjects in which they are allowed to speak freely.

meze
An array of small dishes or dips served as appetizers in many UAE restaurants; a Lebanese tradition.

sharaf
The Bedu code of honor.

souk
A marketplace found in North Africa or the Middle East.

Trucial States
The unofficial union of the emirates formed by the Perpetual Truce, arranged by Great Britain.

unilateral
Involving only one group.

FOR FURTHER INFORMATION

BOOKS

Hashim, Alamira Reem Bani. *Planning Abu Dhabi: An Urban History*. New York, NY: Routledge, Taylor & Francis Group, 2019.

McCarthy, Cecilia Pinto. *Engineering Burj Khalifa*. Minneapolis, MN: Core Library, an Imprint of Abdo Publishing, 2018.

Osier, Peter. *Islamic Art and Architecture*. New York, NY: Britannica Educational Publishing, 2018.

Wolff, Ariana. *The Islamic World from 1041 to the Present*. New York, NY: Britannica Educational Publishing, 2018.

WEBSITES

CIA. *The World Factbook*. "United Arab Emirates." www.cia.gov/the-world-factbook/countries/united-arab-emirates/.

Embassy of the United Arab Emirates in Washington, D.C. www.uae-embassy.org/.

United Arab Emirates Government Portal. u.ae/en.

U.S. Department of State. "United Arab Emirates." www.state.gov/countries-areas/united-arab-emirates/.

BIBLIOGRAPHY

Camerapix. *United Arab Emirates*. Brooklyn, NY: Interlink Publishing Group, 2002.

CIA. *The World Factbook*. "United Arab Emirates." www.cia.gov/the-world-factbook/countries/united-arab-emirates/.

Davidson, Christopher M. *Dubai: The Vulnerability of Success*. New York, NY: Columbia University Press, 2008.

Embassy of the United Arab Emirates. https://www.uae-embassy.org/.

Kechichian, Joseph A., editor. *A Century in Thirty Years: Shaykh Zayed and the United Arab Emirates*. Middle East Policy Council, 2000.

Peterson, J. E., and Jill Ann Crystal. "United Arab Emirates." Britannica Academic. academic.eb.com/levels/collegiate/article/United-Arab-Emirates/110509.

Seznec, Jean-François, and Samer Mosis. *The Financial Markets of the Arab Gulf: Power, Politics and Money*. New York, NY: Routledge Taylor & Francis Group, 2019.

Ulrichsen, Kristian Coates. *The United Arab Emirates: Power, Politics and Policymaking*. New York, NY: Routledge Taylor & Francis Group, 2017.

United Arab Emirates Government. https://u.ae/en.

Wolff, Arianna. *The Islamic World to 1041*. New York, NY: Britannica Educational Publishing, 2018.

INDEX

INDEX